D1336776

TESTAMENT

THE ANIMATED BIBLE

TESTAMENT

THE ANIMATED BIBLE

STORIES FROM THE OLD TESTAMENT

Adapted by Sally Humble-Jackson

■ sapling   S4C~

Testament: The Animated Bible is a multinational venture conceived by S4C (Channel Four Wales). Produced in Russia, Wales and England, the series has been financed by S4C and the BBC (UK), and Christmas Films (Russia). *Testament* has the endorsement of the Bible Society.

First published in Great Britain in 1996 by Boxtree Limited

Text © Sally Humble-Jackson/S4C 1996
Illustrations © S4C/Christmas Films 1996

The right of Sally Humble-Jackson to be identified as Author of this Work has been asserted by her in accordance with the Copyright, Designs and Patents Act 1988.

1 3 5 7 9 10 8 6 4 2

All rights reserved. Except in the United States of America this book is sold subject to the condition that it shall not, by way of trade or otherwise, be lent, resold, hired out or otherwise circulated without the publisher's prior consent in any form of binding or cover other than that in which it is published and without a similar condition including this condition being imposed upon a subsequent purchaser.

Designed by Clare Truscott
Printed and bound in Italy for

Boxtree Limited
Broadwall House
21 Broadwall
London   SE1 9PL

A CIP catalogue entry for this book is available from the British Library.

ISBN 1 85283 0 7522 1041 6

Jacket illustrations courtesy of S4C/Christmas Films/Cartŵn Cymru

The publishers would like to thank Derek Hayes of Cartŵn Cymru for the series title and Eliza Trimby for developing the logo illustration.

CONTENTS

Animation director for 'Creation and the Flood':
Yuri Kulakov of Christmas Films, Moscow
Illustrations by Yuri Kulakov and Victor Chuguevski

Animation director for 'Abraham':
Natalia Dabizha of Christmas Films, Moscow
Photography by Alexander Vikhansky

Animation director for 'Joseph':
Aida Ziablikova of Christmas Films, Moscow
Photographs by Konstantin Ineshin

Animation director for 'Moses':
Gary Hurst of Cartŵn Cymru, Cardiff

Animation director for 'David and Saul':
Gary Hurst of Cartŵn Cymru, Cardiff

Animation director for 'Jonah':
Valeri Ugarov of Christmas Films, Moscow

Animation director for 'Ruth':
Galena Beda of Christmas Films, Moscow
Photography by Alexander Vikhansky

Animation director for 'Elijah':
Derek Hayes of Cartŵn Cymru, Cardiff

Animation director for 'Daniel':
Lucia Koshkina of Christmas Films, Moscow
Illustrations by Lucia Koshkina

Series Editors:
Martin Lamb and Penelope Middelboe,
Right Angle, Tenby, Wales

Producers:
Naomi Jones (Cartŵn Cymru)
Elizabeth Babakhina (Christmas Films)

Associate Producers (BBC):
John Geraint
Geoffrey Marshall-Taylor

Series Executive Producer:
Christopher Grace (S4C)

CREATION
AND THE FLOOD

N o wonder the animals were afraid. They were being hunted from two directions. From the west came a horde of armed riders, bloodthirsty, vicious, cold. From the east came a young man on foot, calling the creatures by name, coaxing, cajoling. The animals did not know who to fear the most.

They knew that the armed men brought death – they had seen it many times. They understood the brightness of metal, the silence of arrows, the pain of wounded flesh. They knew the evil that mankind brought.

But the unarmed man seemed to be beckoning them to something worse; something endless and cramped, dark and dirty, alien and strange.

Arrows were shot. Animals screamed. As blood drenched the forest floor, the animals fled towards the man with the outstretched hand.

The animals were being hunted by a bloodthirsty horde of armed riders.

The grinning soldiers turned back to the city, eager to return to other pleasures, other cruelties. The governor, however, reined in his steed and surveyed the distant plain.

'Look,' jeered his captain, 'there's Noah – building his ship in the middle of dry land.'

'Is he dangerous?' the governor asked.

'He's a fool.'

The governor narrowed his eyes and studied the distant muddle of scaffolding and land-locked ship. 'Let's go and talk to him,' he said menacingly.

The enormous ship was almost finished. Shem and Japhet, the eldest of Noah's three sons, were up on the roof hammering in the last few nails.

'Will it really happen, Shem?' Japhet asked doubtfully.

Shem shrugged. 'I don't know. But *we* don't hear what God says, and Father has never been wrong.'

'But for God to drown the whole world...?'

Noah overheard them and stepped out of the cabin on to the deck. He looked up at his sons.

'God is just,' he explained. 'He may weep at what is required, but He has left plenty of time for repentance.'

'How much time is left?' Japhet asked.

'The Lord God knows that, not me. But if His creation is corrupt, hasn't He the right to put an end to it?'

'So...we should not question the Lord God?'

'By all means question!' Noah said. 'But obey when the answer is clear, even if it is not to your liking.'

The young men pondered their father's words as they continued to work.

'Ham has not come back....' Shem said uneasily.

Japhet sighed. 'How can he bring every wild beast from the

forest to the ark? By magic?'

'Noah!'

Noah looked down from the deck of the towering ship. He had been expecting the two men, had seen their flaming torch bobbing through the dusk.

'Have you no respect for your governor,' the captain said, annoyed that Noah had not rushed down to greet them.

'I will have respect for him when he has respect for my God,' Noah called back.

'You do realize, Noah,' said the governor, 'what I could do to you?'

'I know what you have done to many others, and I know what God will do to you.'

'Ah yes,' sneered the governor, 'the drowning, the black engulfing waters. Is it not possible that you could be mistaken?'

'I am a man. Yes, I could be mistaken. But God – no.'

'Oh, of course, God speaks to you…and says…?'

'He says that you have brought destruction upon yourselves, that you are envious, murderous, adulterous and cruel.'

'And what do you say?'

'I say nothing. I listen.'

With a scornful laugh the two men turned away. As they cantered off the captain threw his torch at the wooden ark. Ham's wife, Atarah, hurtled down through the winding passages of the ark to the ground, snatching the torch away from the hull before it caught fire.

On the ride back to the city the two men schemed to capture the women of Noah's family to punish Noah for his insolence. So engrossed were they that they did not notice the animals at first. But when they did look up, the blood curdled in their veins.

Coming towards them in their thousands were the very beasts they had hunted so mercilessly just hours before. Lions and panthers, bears and elephants, bison and gazelle came stampeding across the plain. The two men spurred their steeds to a gallop and fled, too terrified to understand that the animals were not pursuing them but instead were heading for the ramp which led into the ark.

In their midst, wearing a look of utter amazement, came Ham.

'Father, Father, they came!' he cried. 'Yesterday, the birds and insects and all the small creatures were difficult, unwilling…. But these…. Ha! Look at them now!'

Ham brought all the animals to the ark.

Inside the ark, the animals were settled in their stalls.

It was well into the night before the last animals were settled in their stalls. Noah rested his elbows on the table which stood in the centre of the family's small cabin. The candle flickered.

'It is finished then?' asked Naamah.

Noah smiled at his wife. 'From tomorrow the world will shrink to this wooden shell, you and I, and Shem, Japhet and Ham with their wives.' He took her hand, then turned to his sons. 'Where are they?'

'Feeding the animals.'

'Then we'll water them, Ham, eh?'

The two men set off for the water trough through the dark, narrow corridors of the ark.

'So the world will begin again with us,' Ham said wonderingly.

'By the grace of God,' Noah acknowledged.

'How did it start? I mean, at the very beginning?'

They turned into a passage which no light penetrated. 'At first there was nothing.' Noah's voice echoed in the pitch black. 'Emptiness for ever and ever. And this same darkness still surrounds the earth.'

Ham shivered slightly. He was relieved when they reached the great water tank.

'The spirit of God', breathed Noah, 'hovered over the waters.'

Ham stared at the black surface of the water, awed by the immensity of the vision his father was painting.

'And God said, "Let there be light."'

Beyond the water a golden pin-prick appeared, growing larger as Naamah approached with a small lamp. Ham took the lamp from his mother, astounded at the idea that there had once been a time before light.

'The spirit of God hovered over the waters,' Noah explained.

'And God divided the light from the darkness,' continued Noah. 'One He called day, the other night. And that was the end of the first day.'

Then Noah took up a bucket and dipped it into the water, sending ripples bounding across the surface. 'Next,' he said, lifting the overflowing pail high into the air, 'God divided the waters, those that were under the heavens from those that were above. And that was the end of the second day.'

Ham looked out, away from the trough to the great centre of the ark, where tier upon tier of animals slept. 'And...then the stars

appeared?'

Noah shook his head.

'But look….' Ham pointed into the black space, where thousands of stars seemed to shine.

Noah smiled. 'Bring the light closer.'

In the lamplight the twinkling stars were revealed as the sparkling eyes of a thousand birds.

They were just about to turn away when the birds began to stir uneasily.

'They are afraid of the light…' suggested Ham.

'No.' Noah tilted his head and listened. He could hear rain pattering on the roof of the ark. 'The waters above the heavens,' he announced. 'The Lord God has unloosed them.'

God's rain had begun to fall. The pattering turned to a thundering, the thundering to a roar. Rain slashed through the air, hammered the earth, beat violently on bare rock. Water surged through crevices in mountains, fountained up from the very earth itself. Streams became torrents, fields became lakes, rivers became seas.

Noah and his family battened themselves inside the ark and watched fearfully as the waters heaved and bucked against the scaffold that held the boat erect. The floodwaters rose higher than trees, higher than houses. The mighty ark towered above it all and still the waters deepened, until at last the scaffold splintered and the great ungainly ark began to float.

Day after day the grey clouds cast down their rain. Inside the ark Noah's family tended the animals and waited. Ham stared from the deck at the flat, grey world. No hills. No trees. No people. His heart ached.

'Twenty days and still it rains,' said Atarah, coming to join him.

The rain beat down and the flood water rose higher.

'We are gliding over the highest mountain,' Noah brushed rainwater from his eyes.

'If only I could understand the beginning,' said Ham wearily, 'I might understand this ending.'

'You stopped your story at the end of the second day,' Atarah said eagerly to Noah. She shivered as she remembered Ham telling her about the time before light. Noah thought for a minute, then he pointed at the foggy horizon. 'Had there been an eye to see it, at the dawn of the third day this is how the earth would have appeared. Then the Lord God gathered the waters together and said, "Let the dry land appear."'

Ham and Atarah stared at the formless water, willing it to part as it had done on that third day, willing it to seethe and swirl and throw up dry land.

'At His command', explained Noah, 'the earth brought forth grass and herbs and flowers and trees.'

Tears stung Atarah's eyes. She remembered the sweet fragrance of grass, the bright colours of flowers. Would she ever see such things again?

'Then,' continued Noah softly, 'night fell on the third day. At dawn on the fourth day there was already a new creation. The sun.'

Noah opened his palms to the grey sky as if to find the lost rays. 'The sun warmed and fed the land, like God Himself. And when the evening came on the fourth day, the Lord God unveiled the stars and sailed the moon out between the clouds.'

But there was no window in the sky now for the ghostly moon. There were only clouds weeping raindrops which pricked the endless sea.

'And on the fifth day?' Ham prompted.

'God said, "Let the waters bring forth living creatures that move and have life."'

Ham hung over the edge of the boat and tried to see fishes in the gloomy grey sea.

'By the evening, the sky too was alive with living creatures. And on the sixth day,' said Noah, 'God made the living creatures that live on the earth.'

Atarah put her hands to her cheeks and sighed. There had once been so many creatures – herds of oxen, flocks of starlings, swarms of ants. Now there were just two of each, huddled together in the ark.

'To crown His work,' Noah went on, 'God said, "I will create man and woman. Let them be made in the image of God, their creator."'

Ham took Atarah's hands and kissed them.

'Adam and Eve were created to revel in God,' Noah announced. 'To rule the earth and its creatures, to love and enjoy each other for ever.'

Atarah buried her face against her husband's chest and smiled. 'And on the seventh day?' she asked.

'God rested, as we shall do,' Noah said, wryly. 'But first we must care for our animals.'

Day after day after day passed, and the waters were still rising. Time and again Noah's family begged him to describe paradise, as if by imagining that enchanted place they could keep despair at bay.

And then one day the rain stopped.

'I wonder if there is any dry land showing?' Naamah said.

Noah set a raven free. 'If it does not find land it can come back to roost.'

'Then let's hope he finds land,' muttered Naamah. 'Nasty creature. Deserves to be cast out…like Lucifer from Heaven.'

Noah set a raven free.

'Ah…Lucifer,' muttered Noah, remembering. 'He had a part

in the story of creation, too.'

Then Noah told the young people how Lucifer had once been God's brightest angel – until pride tempted him to challenge God for the highest place of all. Lucifer's heart became black with jealousy and hatred. Evil grew inside him, his splendour dimmed, darkened, until at last he was banished to that blackest place of all – the scalding pit of hell.

When the raven did not return, Noah sent out a dove.

When the raven failed to return, Noah sent out a dove.

'Free!' exclaimed Ham, watching her fly away. 'Though she may come back to the ark.'

Adam and Eve were happy in the garden of Eden.

'Back to prison?' Atarah mocked. 'Is prison part of freedom?'

Noah nodded. 'True freedom always has restraints. There was always a path not taken. Even in paradise...'

'Tell me,' urged Ham.

So Noah told them how Adam and Eve had once been entirely free. The garden of Eden was a perfect world, in which even the tiger was their friend. In the cool of the evening, God would walk with them and speak to them. They were wonderfully happy. They had everything they needed – fruit grew on trees and clear water sparkled in brooks. The only thing they were forbidden was the fruit of a certain tree which God had created.

'It is the tree of all knowledge,

'It is the tree of all knowledge,' said God.

evil as well as good,' God said. 'Bite into that fruit and on that day Death will begin to hunt you down.'

Adam and Eve looked at it with horror. Why on earth would they want to eat that fruit? They could not imagine doing such a thing....

Lucifer surveyed the paradise around him.

But someone else could imagine it. In the scorching depths of hell Lucifer was mustering his strength. At last, with an enormous force of will, he broke the power of the searing flames and surged up through the blackness and into the light.

He spread his arms wide and surveyed the paradise in which he found himself. 'I am the son of the morning,' he snarled. 'I will not dance at the throne of God...I will topple it!'

Then Lucifer shrivelled and shrank until he had become a scaly dragon, a black serpent. He flicked his forked tongue between his rigid lips and looked around him with glittering red eyes. The woman whom God had made...now, where was she?

Eve was alone. She walked happily through the garden of Eden, looking for Adam.

The serpent lay in wait.

'Eve...' he drawled admiringly as she passed him. 'Eve...my child....'

Eve beamed at him. Every day there was something

As the serpent spoke to her, Eve began to feel a strong temptation to taste the forbidden fruit.

wonderful and new to be seen in the garden. 'You are the serpent!' she exclaimed.

'And you are the loveliest thing in a perfect garden – if only you knew it….'

'I do know it now,' Eve laughed. 'You have told me.'

The serpent stretched lazily in the sun. He kept his red, mesmerizing eyes fixed on Eve's innocent face. 'Will you pick some fruit for us?' he asked.

Eve offered him a fragrant peach which she held in her hand. 'Not that….'

'What then?'

The serpent shrugged. He looked around carelessly. 'Something…ah…something rare and delicate…. Look, there in the middle!'

Eve looked at the tree with alarm. 'No,' she said.

'No?' The serpent's eyes clouded with surprise. 'But…doesn't it make your mouth water?'

'We may pick any of the fruits of the garden,' Eve explained gently, 'except those. The Lord God has forbidden us.'

Now the serpent's eyes widened in astonishment. 'If God forbids this or that, Eden is no better than a prison.'

'Oh no,' Eve protested. 'We are free.'

'If God has said you are free, then *be* free.' The serpent's shape remained constant, but now his breath changed into something misty, something red and tempting which seemed to curl around Eve and capture her. 'Pick and eat,' he said.

'If we eat the fruit we will die…' Eve said uncertainly. She could feel the invisible cloak of temptation wrapping around her, making her feel warm and safe.

'You will not die. Death is a big word…. You don't understand it. But you *could* understand everything. Don't you want to be like the God you love so much?'

'Like God...yes, but....'

'But you would rather be a slave?' The serpent's breath grew hotter, became a thick crimson blanket of yearning.

As the serpent continued to wheedle, Eve found herself drawn towards the forbidden tree. Yes...the serpent must be right...surely....

Eve's hand reached up to the beautiful fruit.

Her hand reached up and plucked one of the beautiful fruits. It smelled wonderful. She put it to her mouth and bit into the flesh.

Red juice trickled through her fingers like blood. She looked at it, bemused. The serpent's breath stroked her neck, reassuring, convincing. Yes...she *had* been right to eat it....

A bird flew up, startling her. Suddenly she felt horribly alone. Oh, how she wished Adam would eat this fruit as well.... She could not bear this feeling of loneliness.

She ran to Adam with the half-eaten fruit in her hand. He looked at her in horror. This was Eve...his Eve.... But she seemed different, distant, unreachable. He bit into the fruit, knowing that it would bring them together again.

The moment he had eaten, the fruit rotted in his hand. He threw it down in disgust. Then he shivered. For the first time ever, Adam felt shame. He could not bear to look at Eve nor down at himself. He had no name for this sickening feeling in his stomach, this scorching of his skin, but he did know that Eve and he were no longer the perfect creatures that God had made. They were spoiled. For ever.

'We must cover ourselves,' Adam said in dismay. 'We are naked.'

The listeners touched their faces, appalled. How could Lucifer have been so cruel? And how could Adam and Eve have done such a thing?

But Noah did not explain.

'Why have you stopped?' they clamoured.

'Can't you feel it?'

It came again. It was the rasp of keel on dry land. The family rushed to look out. The water was seeping away.

'One day soon, by God's grace,' said Noah gratefully, 'you will smell hay, warm earth...'

'Fresh timber,' added Shem.

Naamah touched her sleeve. There would be new cloth, clean wool.... 'And will we ever eat fish or fig-bread again?'

The others laughed delightedly.

'Never!' cried Japhet.

'Look!' exclaimed Ham, pointing at the dove, who was flying back to them with an olive twig in her beak.

'The long days are nearly over,' Noah said, his voice thick with emotion. 'There is land somewhere close.'

'Finish your story while the flood drains away,' urged Shem. 'Please…'

'What did God do to them?'

'He kept His promise,' said Noah, 'He gave them what they, in their freedom, had chosen. Cruelty and death.'

Ham remembered the frightened animals gathering around him, the arrows slicing through the air, the smell of blood. Yes, God had indeed sent cruelty and death into the world.

The dove returned to the ark bearing an olive twig.

Then Noah told them how, for the first time, Adam and Eve experienced fear. The fabulous garden was suddenly full of danger. The animals had become menacing, the sun burned too hot, the smell of death was in the air.

Adam and Eve had spoiled God's perfect creation. Thorns sprang up, beast turned against beast, disease floated in on the wind.

Frightened and ashamed, Adam and Eve seemed to stand alone against the world.

And yet they knew that God was watching them, that God saw. They covered themselves with leaves to hide their nakedness and hid in a cave.

Then God came to them. 'Adam, Eve, tell me why you are hiding,' He said sadly.

'We are naked,' Adam mumbled.

'You have always been naked,' God reminded them. 'Why

Adam and Eve
were cast out of
paradise.

are you ashamed?' He sighed. 'You have eaten of the fruit. My single commandment – and you have broken it.'

'The serpent reasoned with me,' Eve protested. 'He made me listen.'

'We had no arguments,' accused Adam.

'I did not give you the burden of understanding, only of obedience.'

Eve groaned. 'Something has gone,' she cried. 'Something I knew.'

'That,' said God, 'is a pain that you – and your children – will never shed. The pain you now feel is the mirror of mine.'

Then the evil serpent crept into view.

'Shape-shifter! I know you!' blazed God damningly. 'Hunt and be hunted! Crawl for ever in the dust....'

At God's words the serpent's skin began to blister and crack. From it slithered a snake. The creature crawled through the dust, away from his empty skin, his abandoned claws.

'I made you a world,' God said to Adam and Eve. 'Now make your own.'

Adam and Eve looked at one another in despair. They had already made their world....

'Will you curse me when it has no purpose?' asked God. 'No beauty?'

Tears sprang to their eyes. They knew the difference between beauty and ugliness now, between good and evil, innocence and guilt. If they strived, strived all the days of their lives, could they create perfection with their own hands? Could they ever lose their shame?

'Now you know shame,' said God, 'you must put on skins.'

Adam and Eve hung their heads. Oh, what had they done?

'There is consolation...' God encouraged, '...in all that lies unused in your hearts. There will always be the memory of a

memory. And there will be a way back.'

'Are we the way?' asked Naamah as she stepped out of the ark on to the damp earth.

'We may be part of it,' said Noah, hopefully. He took his wife's arm. 'You are as beautiful to me as Eve must have been to Adam.'

'And you are the oldest man on earth!' laughed Ham. 'Adam again! Tell me, does the fruit still exist?'

'Listen. The fruit had no power, no magic. It was the commandment that was important.'

'And because the commandment was so easy to keep,' said Atarah thoughtfully, 'the punishment was made so hard to bear.'

'You have a wise wife, Ham,' Noah said admiringly. 'Eat the fruit she offers you.'

When an altar to the Lord God had been built the animals were set free. Ham watched them racing away, thousands upon thousands of them, searching for new homes.

'Will this world ever be home for us?'

'We are always drawn to home,' said Noah wisely. 'But you have heard the story. Home must be in heaven now, not anywhere on earth.'

'But...but what if the floods return?'

Noah did not answer. Ham's question hung in the air.

And then God answered; His voice echoed in the silence of the new-made world.

'Settle in the land I have given back to you. Never again will I destroy the earth with floods, but rain will give way to sun, and you will see my promise in the clouds.'

They all looked up. Even the animals, in all their hurry, stopped in their tracks to gaze at the sky.

High above them
was God's promise
– a rainbow.

There, high above them, was God's promise. It was a rainbow, God's newest creation. Shimmering, iridescent, radiant – all the colours of paradise swept down from heaven to touch the earth.

ABRAHAM

Every morning the women of Haran would grind their corn.

Sarah always finished first. She only needed to grind enough to make bread for her husband and herself. The women who had children had to work much harder, but even so, not one of them envied Sarah. Hard work was a very small price to pay for a child's love.

As Abraham watched Sarah tend to a neighbour's little girl, his heart ached. 'Children love you, Sarah,' he said sadly.

'They love us both,' his wife acknowledged with tears in her eyes. 'But they will never call you "Father". No one will.'

Abraham and Sarah longed for a child of their own.

When the sun went down, the people of Haran called their little ones indoors and laughed and sang together as they settled the children for the night.

Sarah lit the lamp and busied herself in the house while Abraham went outdoors to walk in the cool evening air, away from the city into the desert beyond. 'When we are dead,' he murmured, 'the moon will visit still, the tribes will leave their footprints in the sand, new cities will rise. And still, childless men will wonder what will fasten on their names when they have died.'

The stars above seemed to shiver in sympathy. The dry wind seemed to cry out his name.

'Abraham….'

He started at the unexpected sound.

'Who is it?' he demanded softly, looking up at the night sky.

'I am the Lord your God.'

'The Lord?' Abraham whispered, his heart thundering. 'A God speaks to me?' Could this be the God of his forefathers, the God who had created the world and flooded it long ago?

'Leave this place,' commanded God. 'I have claimed a land for you.'

Abraham frowned.

'A land for your son to inherit,' the Lord God replied.

Abraham could not speak for a long moment. 'A son?' he echoed at last. '*A son for me and Sarah?* Is it not too late for us?'

'Uproot from the past. Begin afresh. I will take you where you belong.'

Abraham trembled as he hurried back to the city. A son! After all these years! How he and Sarah had longed for a child.

Abraham's voice shook as he told his wife what had happened.

But Sarah's heart sank when she heard that a child was

promised. Year in, year out, she had hoped for a baby, but her hopes had brought nothing but disappointment. Her pain had only eased when she had finally stopped dreaming.

She did not want to believe this God who spoke to Abraham,

because she did not want to start hoping again.

When everything was at last ready, Abraham led his servants and his shepherds, his nephew and his nephew's family, his camels and his sheep out of Haran towards the distant land of Canaan.

They left the cool city with light hearts, but once they were out in the scorching desert, they began to have doubts. Why on earth would the Lord God want them to leave a prosperous place like Haran to make their home in the wilderness?

And then, right in the heart of the desert, God spoke to Abraham again.

'You are a tiny seed', He said, 'that will blossom into a nation that will know me and love me. You will be father to my own people, and I will be their God for ever.'

Abraham looked around him in wonder.

'This empty wilderness will swarm with your descendants — as many as the sand grains under your feet.'

'I can count a million million grains of sand,' said the bewildered Abraham, 'but no children. You know how we have yearned. It is too late for Sarah now.'

But God was adamant. 'You will outnumber the stars in the sky, the dust on the earth. This land is yours.'

'This is God's will,' Abraham insisted when the sun grew too hot, when the water-skins ran dry, when his sheep and his nephew's sheep had to share the same few withered leaves. 'It is the right thing to do.'

And so they kept trudging on, through the heat of the day, through suffocating sandstorms, across acres of blistering rock.

But Abraham's nephew, Lot, was a headstrong young man.

'A place for men to starve and go mad,' he grumbled as they trailed across yet more barren land. 'Is this the future you promised?' He blinked dust out of his eyes. The desert wind was getting up, swirling sand into the air. 'Have we left our cushions, our cool walks, our gardens, for this?'

The sheep staggered in the sun. Sweat ran down Sarah's brow. Even the camel on which she rode sweltered beneath her. 'Lot is right,' she groaned. 'Why have you led us to this bone-bare wilderness?'

'Sarah, beloved,' returned Abraham patiently, 'I have often been wrong. But now *God* has spoken. I choose as God chooses. God knows best. We must trust Him.'

Lot rolled his eyes. God might very well want Abraham to live out his days in the desert – but if God wanted Lot there too, then why had He not said so?

'What was wrong with prosperity and comfort?' Lot said. 'Ha! Give me something to tell the sheep.'

But Abraham could not relent.

'Sour rock and bleached grass,' Lot muttered, stooping to help a fallen animal. 'The sheep fight for every blade.'

'But we should not fight,' said Abraham.

'Your decisions always have to be mine,' said Lot bitterly.

Abraham shook his head. 'Lot, choose your path, left or right,' he offered, pointing through the dancing sand at the horizon. 'And I will take the other.'

'Then I choose the Jordan valley and the city of Sodom. I have a wife, children. I cannot sacrifice them to a dream.'

'May you prosper,' shouted Abraham into a wind which snatched his words away. 'Sarah and I will go on into Canaan.'

As Lot and his family disappeared into the storm, Sarah bit her lip. 'Lot has taken the valley,' she said enviously. 'Lush and green with wells! Oh, Abraham! Canaan is withered and shrivelled by the sun.'

Lot did not want to follow his uncle into the desert.

Abraham and
Sarah made their
new home in
the mountains of
Canaan.

'But this land is holy,' her husband responded. 'Our children will inherit it.'

Sarah looked away. Surely Abraham, in his yearning for a son, had misunderstood God's meaning? It was too late for children now.

The mountains of Canaan were beautiful to the eye, but difficult to farm. Time after time the sheep needed fresh grazing, which meant that the huddle of tents had to be moved, too. Their life was harder than it had ever been.

And there was, after all, no child.

Sarah smoothed grey hairs back from her brow and sighed dispiritedly as she surveyed the encampment. To think that this was now her home! 'We are blown like rattling leaves from desert to desert,' she complained.

'We must risk all that we love,' Abraham explained, 'to find a greater safety in God's love.'

Sarah looked away with weary eyes.

'Sarah,' persisted Abraham eagerly, 'He promised us a son!'

Sarah let out a hopeless moan. 'You know I can never bear a child, and yet you and your God taunt me with it.'

'He has promised.'

'He speaks to *you* – of *your* descendants,' Sarah replied miserably. She frowned at the pitiful little camp, pitched in an endless waste of sand. Her servant came out from one of the tents to wash dishes. Poor Hagar. Life was not easy for her, either.

Sarah watched as Hagar's smooth, vigorous hands rubbed briskly at a brass plate. She looked at Hagar's unlined face and her glossy black curls.

'Hagar is young,' murmured Sarah, thoughtfully. 'And she is kind.' She took a deep breath. 'Perhaps she will make you a father.'

Abraham was shocked. 'No, Sarah, I am yours!' he exclaimed. 'You are the one I love.'

But Sarah was not listening. 'This must be the way,' she insisted. 'Hagar belongs to me.... Any child of hers will be mine. That is the law.'

Sarah loved her husband dearly and wanted him to have his son more than anything in the world. At last she persuaded him that this must be God's will. She made up her mind not to be jealous. She would be happy, always, for his sake.

Hagar grew round
with Abraham's child.

Hagar was happy too. Abraham's child would be lord of all Canaan one day – but first he would be her darling baby! She would love him with all her heart.

Before long Hagar grew round as Sarah had yearned to grow round. And as Sarah watched Hagar swell with Abraham's child, all the old longings returned.

When Hagar grew tired, Sarah's limbs grew heavy with yearning. When Hagar laid her hand on her belly, Sarah clenched her fists in front of her face to hide her hunger for a child of her own. When Hagar sat dreamily in the sun, Sarah imagined how it must feel to have a baby inside you, waiting to be born, and her heart ached as terribly as it had done all those years ago.

Sarah grew jealous, despite her promise to herself.

'Hagar,' Sarah said sharply, seeing Hagar admiring herself in the mirror. 'Are you tired? Have you done your work?'

'Does it matter? I've certainly done yours.' Hagar smiled lazily, scarcely aware of what she had just said.

Sarah let out a cry of dismay.

'Oh no!' Hagar clapped her hand guiltily to her mouth. 'I'm so sorry!'

'You dare to say that!' shouted Sarah. 'Out! Get out!'

Hagar took one look at her mistress' face and fled into the wilderness.

As soon as she had gone Sarah was appalled by what she had done. Hearing her crying, Abraham rushed to her side.

'Sarah,' he gasped. 'What have you done?'

She turned desperate eyes on her husband. 'For months I have watched her growing big with your child,' she sobbed. 'I held my tongue. But now…oh, now I have spilt our future into the desert.'

Abraham held out his hand to Sarah. 'She must come back,' he said kindly. 'Can God's promises be broken?'

Hagar stumbled blindly through the burning sand, sobbing with fear. How could she survive out here in this terrible desert? What would happen to her child? Panic-stricken, she fell to the ground.

In the wilderness, a stranger came to Hagar.

'Hagar!'

She froze. Who was calling her name?

'Hagar! Return to Sarah.'

She looked over her shoulder. A man was gazing down on her, guarding her, a man dressed all in white, his back to the blazing sun so that she could not see his face.

'Do not be afraid,' said the figure. 'She will be kind.'

Hagar covered her face with her hands.

'And you will bear a son,' the man

continued. 'A son who will grow to be a man fierce and passionate, and one who will stir passions. Ishmael will be the father of a great nation.'

As the figure dissolved into the sunlight, Hagar understood that she was being guarded by an angel of God. Overwhelmed, she got to her feet and began to retrace her steps.

When Hagar arrived back at the camp Sarah was indeed kind. And when the time came for the birth, Sarah did everything for Hagar's comfort.

As soon as the tiny boy was safely born, Sarah gathered him in her arms. According to the law this was her son – but when the infant stretched out his hand to Hagar, Sarah understood that he would never really be hers.

'Look, Abraham!' Sarah managed to keep the disappointment out of her voice as she handed the little bundle to his father. 'Our son! Name him.'

'My son is named already,' burst out Hagar. 'The angel breathed it – Ishmael.'

Sarah gathered the baby in her arms.

'Ishmael!' echoed Abraham proudly, gazing with love at the crumpled, newborn face. 'My son!'

As Abraham watched Hagar with the child, he wondered whether this was truly the son whom God had promised? He touched the baby's little fist. No matter. Whoever Ishmael should turn out to be, he would be loved.

Ishmael was a fortunate child. He had three parents who loved him. And, as the years went by, he grew strong and tall. He played for hours with his bow and arrow until he could shoot as well as any man. And when the tents were loaded on to camels and a new part of the desert found for the sheep, he often ran ahead, faster than the shepherd boys and certainly faster than his ageing father.

And then one day, while Abraham sat in the shadow of a tree and Ishmael played, three strangers approached the tents.

'Look, Father!'

Abraham struggled to his feet and went forward to greet the visitors. As they came nearer he shaded his eyes to see them better. They were dressed and hooded in white – but he could not see their faces for the glare of the sun.

Three strangers approached the tent.

'Welcome, my lords.' Abraham said, bowing his head. He gestured at the tree. 'Sit for a while in the shade and then eat with me.'

'Your wife, Sarah?' queried the foremost of the men as Hagar and Ishmael brought food and drink.

'She is in the tent,' said Abraham vaguely. Surely he had heard that voice before?

'I shall come again with springtime, Abraham.'

Abraham's heart lurched. *This was the voice of the Lord God!*

'Sarah shall bear you a son. He will live to be a father to God's people.'

Hidden inside the tent, Sarah laughed a silent, bitter laugh. 'A son?' she muttered. 'Who taunts me now? My body is old. It is too late.'

'Why laughter, Sarah?' asked the stranger. 'Is anything impossible for God?'

Sarah's blood froze. Who was this stranger who promised her a child? *And how did he know that she had laughed?* 'What laughter?' she denied, coming out of the tent to see who this man could be.

'Sarah,' He said, 'I hear beyond silence to the meaning of silence.'

Sarah's heart pounded. Surely no one could hear her silent thoughts?

'Listen to me,' He reassured her. 'Time is mine to speed or slacken. I twist it for you. You shall have the son I promised. Call him Isaac.'

Sarah's hands trembled. A son? Isaac? The name meant laughter – but she no longer felt like mocking the stranger with laughter. Suddenly she trusted this man from the depths of her soul.

'I shall bless you through him,' He said.

This must be the Lord God! Sarah turned to Abraham, her eyes brimming with tears. 'You could always believe,' she whispered. 'Now my belief is sure.'

As God and His two angels departed, God said to Abraham, 'I have chosen you, and to my chosen I reveal secrets. Sodom and Gomorrah rot and reek of sin. Now is the time for the fire of cleansing.'

Abraham was frightened. Lot was in Sodom with his family. 'Lord, will you destroy a city that contains fifty who love you?' he asked anxiously.

'No, for fifty I would spare the city.'

'Lord forgive me, and for ten?'

'Yes, even for ten good people I would spare the rest.'

And then God and his angels melted away.

Abraham sighed. All he could do now was hope. God knew Lot's heart. God would decide....

Lot and his family were no longer happy in Sodom. It had become an evil place. Every time Lot stepped outside his house he saw drunkards leering, women flaunting themselves, youths

The city of Sodom was an evil place.

Two strangers
came to Lot's
door.

sniggering and fighting. Lot feared for his daughters' safety.

When two strangers came to Lot's door, dressed all in white, Lot feared for them, too. While the townsmen caroused in the street, he hurried them indoors and offered them safe lodgings for the night.

'Lot!' they said. 'Bring everyone you care for.'

Lot's wife and his two daughters looked in bewilderment on the men's faces, but there was a brightness which made it impossible for them to see.

'This city tilts on the edge of darkness,' the angels continued. 'Its death is folded in our wings. Fly from the city! Run from your graves! Run! But do not look back – not once!'

Shadowed by the angels' wings, they fled. And as they fled, fire rained down upon Sodom like molten copper. Within minutes the entire city was ablaze. Lot's family could feel the heat on their backs. The flames flickered at the edge of their vision.

'Don't look back,' warned Lot.

But the temptation was too great for his wife. She looked back.

It was the last thing she ever did. First she froze, her face to the city, her expression curious, her eyes shocked. And then slowly she turned into a pillar of salt.

Lot's wife turned into a pillar of salt.

Springtime came to Sarah. Old as she was, she grew round and big. When she realized that God's promise would at last be kept, that she would bear a child, her heart swelled with joy.

And when she held her tiny son in her arms for the first time, she felt she might burst with happiness.

'Oh, Isaac,' she smiled. 'God named you laughter and you have brought it back to life!'

'He is your gift, Lord,' murmured Abraham, glancing from his wife's happy face to the face of his second son. 'Your miracle.'

'He is your gift, Lord!' said Abraham, holding his new son, Isaac.

Hagar wanted
Ishmael to be
Abraham's heir.

Ishmael loved his brother. He was fascinated by the tiny toes, the sleepy eyes.

But Hagar had something more important on her mind. 'Ishmael is your heir, my lord,' she reminded Abraham. 'Give him your blessing.'

Abraham sighed. What Hagar asked was impossible. The Lord God had chosen Isaac.

'Ishmael is the elder, your firstborn,' Hagar protested angrily.

'But Isaac is his father's heir,' returned Sarah, jealous for her baby. She turned to Abraham. 'Send her and the child away,' she demanded.

'No, Sarah!' protested the old man, deeply shocked.

'She is *my* servant,' Sarah muttered. 'I will decide.'

But in the end it was the Lord God who decided. 'Abraham,' He said. 'Listen to Sarah and not your heart. Free them. Let them go. All shall be well with them.'

Hagar and Ishmael walked away, secure in the knowledge that God would care for them. Ishmael would still have the future that God had promised.

The baby changed everything. For Sarah, having a child was like starting life all over again.

Isaac was a spirited child, always full of laughter, always full of fun.

'Mother, Mother, look at me!' he cried, sliding down the hump of a camel as though the solemn animal had been put on the earth just for his entertainment. And even when he fell into the sand he just laughed.

Abraham loved to watch his child at play. How good God was, to bring so much love into this life. And oh, how beautiful was the laughter of God's promised child.

But then the Lord God spoke to Abraham once again.

Isaac brought great joy to Sarah's life.

'Your son, Isaac, you longed for and love.' God said. 'Take him and sacrifice him to me. A burnt offering.'

Abraham's blood ran cold. He fell to his knees. 'No!' he cried hoarsely. He felt as though he were drowning. 'No!'

'A burnt offering,' God insisted.

'Lay down my son in flames?' Abraham's voice cracked with emotion. He began to weep most dreadfully.

'Abraham,' insisted God. 'Surrender him!'

'You trample, you tear me, Lord! Take anything....'

'Abraham. Surrender him.'

Abraham crouched on the ground, weeping. This was the same Lord God in whom he had trusted. This was the Lord God who had saved Lot's children from the flames. *But this was also the Lord God who had to be obeyed.*

'Endless darkness,' Abraham howled. 'It closes over me.'

Abraham's hands shook as he gathered wood and took fire in a crucible from the house to carry with him. His skin grew clammy as he sharpened his knife, away from Sarah's sight. His teeth chattered as he looked around to find his son.

But when he called Isaac over and asked him to carry the firewood, his voice was as steady as a rock. He did not know how he was going to kill his dear little son, but he did know that he would die rather than frighten the child one second before it was necessary.

And then, when everything was ready, Abraham led Isaac to the mountain and the lonely altar.

Sarah could not understand where they had gone. Nor could she understand why she cared so much about their absence. Maybe they were chasing lost sheep? But if so, then why was she so dreadfully afraid?

'Lord God!' she cried. 'Guide them into safety!'

As they trekked up the mountainside Isaac frowned. He had seen sacrifices before, and knew what usually happened. 'Father, we carry fire and wood,' he said. 'But where is the poor creature that must die?'

Abraham's heart was in his mouth. 'God has chosen a lamb,' he said gravely. 'Isaac, listen...and forgive.'

The child walked in silence for a few moments. He looked up at his father's sombre face. 'Am I the lamb the Lord God chooses?' he asked – and he saw the answer in Abraham's eyes.

'Am I a trouble to Him?' he suggested in a puzzled voice.

'It...it is the Lord's command,' explained Abraham.

Bravely the child walked towards the altar. If the Lord commanded it, then it must be done.

'Do it quickly,' begged Isaac as his father bound his wrists. 'I am afraid.' The will to live was pulling at Isaac, trying to make him run away, but he did not give in.

Drawing strength from the boy's courage, Abraham gently laid his dear son upon the dry sticks, almost as though he were settling him for the night.

Isaac did not struggle. He trusted his father – even in this.

Abraham slipped his knife out of his belt with one hand, and with the other he covered Isaac's eyes.

He raised the knife high.

'No, Abraham!' called out the Lord God. 'The boy is not needed. Only the faith that would give him up!'

Abraham dropped the knife on the ground and flung his arms around his child, sobbing with relief.

Abraham raised the knife high.

'Take him,' said God lovingly. 'Take him and walk into the sunlight of your God.'

Abraham thanked God with all his heart as he took Isaac in his arms and set him safely on the ground. Then, finding a ram trapped by thorns close by, he sacrificed the animal to the Lord God as a sign of his immense gratitude.

As father and son made their way home, God watched over them, pleased that they would have surrendered so much for His sake, pleased to have witnessed such faith.

Abraham watched with pride as his son ran ahead. One day Isaac would raise children, would teach them to know God and love Him. God's seed was beginning to blossom.

A nation would indeed be born, a nation that would one day outnumber the stars in the sky.

'From Adam to Abraham,' the old man murmured, 'the Lord God has been patient, waiting. Now God waits for you, Isaac, and your brother Ishmael.'

JOSEPH

I t was different this time. They had picked on him before – in a family of twelve brothers there would always be squabbles – but this time they really seemed to mean it. This time their blows really hurt.

'Look,' complained Joseph, 'it was just a dream…a stupid dream…all right?'

Simeon and Levi grabbed his arms and held him while Judah knelt in front of him. 'No more than ears of corn are we, O mighty one!' Judah mocked. He flopped forward. 'Bending before you in the wind….'

'I didn't say that!' Joseph wailed.

Joseph's brothers grabbed him – they were really angry this time.

'And the sun and the moon and the stars all fell from the sky and landed at your feet, did they?' Judah continued bitterly.

'I didn't say that either.' Joseph struggled to get free. 'Let me go!'

'Of course, O ruler of nations....' jeered Simeon, throwing him to the ground.

'I can't help it if I have dreams,' protested Joseph. 'And I can't help it if they prophesy greatness.'

At that, his nine older brothers, who were out with him tending the sheep, let out a howl of derision. Who did he think he was? It was bad enough when he boasted about being their father's favourite, but now he was claiming that God had singled him out, too!

Judah took Joseph's robe – far more beautiful than the others' robes – and flung it over the branch of a tree to make a swing.

'That was a gift from Father!' Joseph cried.

'Was it really?' taunted Judah as the cloth ripped under his weight.

'You don't know how much it means to me!'

Judah gritted his teeth. 'Oh, I think I do, Joseph. But why don't you tell me for the one hundred thousandth time?' He pulled out his knife to frighten Joseph. 'In case I've missed the point.'

Reuben, the tenth and eldest brother, appeared on horseback at that moment and sighed. 'Don't be a fool, Judah,' he muttered.

Judah eyed him grudgingly. Reuben had not been around to hear Joseph's latest bout of boasting, had not been told he was nothing but an ear of corn in God's eyes.

Reuben raised his eyebrows. He was sick of Joseph, too, but he did not want to get the blame for harming him.

'He has to go, Reuben,' said Judah through clenched teeth.

'So what are you going to do? Cut his throat and have his

blood on your hands for the rest of your days?'

Judah winced. He put his knife away.

Reuben shrugged. 'I tell you what,' he said, turning his horse and moving off. 'Throw him in the pit. At least that way, our hands stay clean.' And later, he thought to himself, he could come and get him out – assuming Judah had not cooled off and done it already.

There was a dry well just yards away. Judah glanced at his brothers.

'I'm Father's favourite, remember....' said Joseph with a quavering voice as his brothers advanced on him.

It was the wrong thing to have said. Joseph had no idea how deeply hurt his brothers were by their father's attitude. Stirred to a jealous rage, the young men rushed at Joseph and pushed him into the pit.

Joseph shouted up from the depths of the pit.

'Is he dead?' Judah asked. But Joseph could be heard crying out from the depths of the pit.

'Good,' said Judah, narrowing his eyes and staring into the distance to where a string of slave traders with their camels could be seen. 'I have an idea. We'll sell him.'

The traders were delighted to buy such a healthy, strong youth. They could get a good price for him if they took him to Egypt. As they set off, Judah looked at the twenty pieces of silver in his hand and shivered.

'What will we tell Father?' Levi whispered.

'Bring me a goat,' Judah said shakily. 'We can kill it, soak Joseph's coat in the blood and tell Father that a mountain lion got him.'

The brothers turned shocked eyes on Judah.

'This will destroy our father.'

The traders were glad to buy Joseph.

'The truth will hurt him ten times more.'

'Oh, if only Joseph's mother hadn't died giving birth to

Benjamin! She would have been able to comfort Father. Rachel was the only one of his wives that he really loved.'

'Little Benjamin will miss him too.'

'First his mother, now his brother...'

'He's still got us.'

'We're only his half-brothers.... It's not the same.'

When they returned home to Jacob and Benjamin, Joseph's brothers explained that he had been killed by a lion.

The traders offered Joseph to Potiphar, the captain of Pharaoh's guard and one of Egypt's most powerful men.

'He smells,' said Potiphar.

'Of course he smells, my lord. We have travelled far. But as you see, he has broad shoulders, strong legs...'

'Yes, yes. They've all got strong legs. My house is full of your

◄ 59 ►

The slave trader brought Joseph before Potiphar… and his wife.

bargains with strong legs.'

Potiphar's beautiful wife shimmered into view. She let her gaze rest lingeringly on Joseph. 'He does have magnificent legs….'

Potiphar rolled his eyes and smiled. 'The legs again, you see? It's always the legs.'

'And a strong back,' consoled his wife.

'Ah, but does he have a brain?' Potiphar asked. 'That's what interests me.'

'I'm afraid not, my lord, no,' Joseph replied.

'I beg your pardon?'

'If I had a brain I would know the meaning of arrogance, and had I known that I wouldn't be here.'

Potiphar hooted with laughter. 'I'll take him!' he exclaimed delightedly. 'He'll go far, that young man.'

'Yes,' said his wife slowly. 'I rather think he might.'

Indeed, Joseph did go far. While his father was grieving endlessly in Canaan, Joseph was prospering in Egypt. Within a couple of years he had become the overseer of all Potiphar's estates.

Potiphar's wife summoned Joseph.

One day he was summoned by Potiphar's wife.

He sighed as he trudged off to her quarters. Potiphar's wife was becoming a bit of a nuisance.

'My husband returns from his trip tomorrow,' she said when he entered her room.

'Everything is in hand for the celebrations,' he reassured her.

'You have always been a favourite of mine, Joseph. I would like to give you something special.' She moved closer, pouting her lips. 'Now, what could that be, do you think?'

Joseph shook his head.

'Could it be me…?' she asked coyly, taking his hand.

Joseph recoiled. 'You are my master's wife,' he protested. 'It would be a sin against God.'

'Do you find me undesirable?' she demanded dangerously.

'You…you are extremely desirable, madam,' Joseph flattered. 'It is only in the power of God that I find the strength to refuse you.'

'Joseph,' she flared, 'I'm losing patience.'

But nothing would make Joseph give in. He pulled away from her and ran. As he hurtled through the door she grabbed a knife and flung it after him, pinning his robe to the door-post. With a jolt he tore the garment free and escaped.

Potiphar's wife was insulted beyond measure. How dare this slave turn her down! How dare he! She snatched the knife in one hand and yelled for the guards at the top of her voice.

'Help me someone!' she screamed. 'I've been attacked.'

Joseph was thrown into the dungeons.

The torn robe seemed proof enough for anyone. Within the hour Joseph had been thrown into the dungeons.

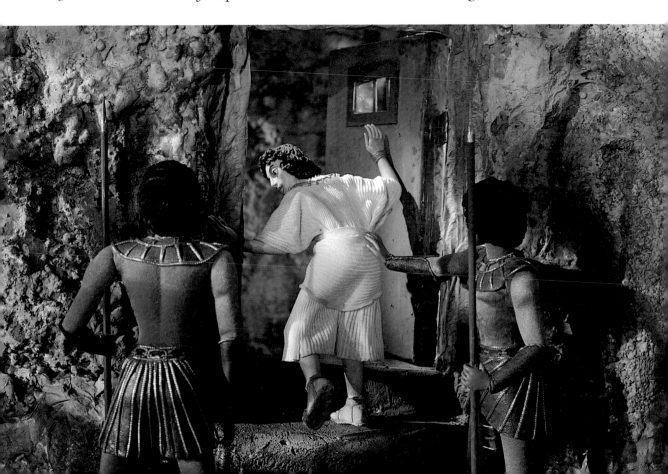

Jacob grieved dreadfully for the son he thought was dead.

Did Jacob, Joseph's father, know of his beloved son's wretchedness that first night in prison? No! How could he have done? Jacob believed Joseph was dead. And the dead could not weep.

But something stirred Jacob that night. Something took the old man out of his tent to sit beneath the cold stars. 'So what if I favoured him?' he accused God. 'He meant more to me than my life. Is that such a sin? You...you promise so much and then take away even more.'

He got to his feet and railed at the velvet sky. 'All I want is the life of the child by the only woman I truly loved. You hear me?' He shook his fists at the sky. 'Just give me back my son.... JOSEPH!'

Joseph's first year in prison stretched endlessly, though with God's help he endured it better than most. And the other captives were company of a sort, though no one could be cheerful in that dank, stinking hole – except the warder, of course.

And then, on Pharaoh's birthday, two prisoners were sent for. They were Pharaoh's butler and his baker. Joseph had known they were going to leave prison because both men had told Joseph their dreams. Joseph's ability to interpret dreams meant that he understood what was going to happen to the men. The butler was going to be given his job back, but the baker was going to be killed.

Jealousy burned inside Joseph as he watched the butler being led to the door. 'Help me, old friend,' he pleaded. 'I beg you. Speak to the Pharaoh for me!'

The butler agreed, but, of course, in all the excitement of being restored to his old life he quickly forgot the promise.

And so Joseph lay in prison, forgotten by everyone except God.

As the years passed, life in Pharaoh's Egypt went on in its usual way. Potiphar's wife bought more slaves with fine legs, Potiphar appointed a new overseer, and the butler worked extra hard to make sure he stayed out of prison.

And then one night the peace of the palace was disturbed by terrible cries. Pharaoh was having a nightmare. He soon went back to sleep but after a while he woke up screaming again.

It happened again the next night. On the third night, Pharaoh woke up yelling, 'The dream! I've had it again! Send me my counsellors and magicians at once.'

'Mighty Pharaoh,' soothed his butler, 'this is the third time in as many nights they have attended you. Is there any point?'

'Find me someone who understands,' sobbed Pharaoh. 'Someone I can trust. Help me, old friend.'

The butler frowned. 'Help me, old friend?' Someone else had said that to him once…a long, long time ago.

And so Joseph was remembered. He was brought to the palace the following day, his head bowed with fear. What on earth did Pharaoh want with him?

When he was told about the dream he shivered with relief. 'The God of my fathers,' he explained respectfully, 'has shown you what is to take place, your Majesty.'

'Go on,' urged Pharaoh.

'The seven fat cows and the seven good ears of corn you saw in your dream refer to seven years of prosperity that will come to this land. The seven thin cows and the seven bad ears of corn that you saw in your dream – which consumed the first seven cows and first ears of corn – they refer to seven years of famine that will follow.'

'And what does this God of your fathers propose that I should do about it?'

'Whatever is wise and prudent.'

'And what might that be?'

'Set stewards over the fields to prepare for the time to come.'

Pharaoh studied Joseph carefully. 'Come here, Joseph.'

Joseph came nearer.

Pharaoh looked into his eyes. 'If you were in my place, would you believe this interpretation?'

'If I were in your place and as wise as you, O Pharaoh, I would know it to be the truth.'

Pharaoh continued to look hard into Joseph's eyes. At last he said, 'Well then. We'd better prepare my people for famine. You can be in charge, Joseph.'

Joseph became a very powerful man. His task was to force all the landowners in Egypt to store half of their crops, ready for the famine. Pharaoh gave him an Egyptian name so that people would know that he had Pharaoh's authority behind him, and great wealth and many servants so that he could impress the farmers with his power. He even gave Joseph a wife! Joseph worked extremely hard; he knew that if he did not, people would starve.

Joseph became a powerful man in Egypt.

At the end of seven years the famine began.

Joseph's work changed. Instead of forcing people to store their grain, he had to begin portioning it out. Everyone was strictly rationed so that the corn in the granaries would last out the seven years. Every day, people who needed extra food would come to see Joseph, knowing that they would be treated fairly.

One day, after three years of famine, his servant Kai checked his list and said, 'There's a family from Canaan next.'

'Canaan?' Joseph's heart jumped. It was many years since he had heard the name of his own country spoken aloud. 'Has the famine spread that far?'

'Further, I'm told.'

'Send them in,' muttered Joseph, thinking of his own family and hoping they had food enough.

But they had not.

And Joseph knew they had not the instant the Canaanites entered the room. He knew it because the ten men who stood before him, pleading to be allowed to buy food, were his own brothers. His mouth went dry, and his heart began to thump heavily.

'My Lord Zaphenath-paneah,' stumbled Reuben, hardly daring to look at the impressive man in the Egyptian headdress. 'Our father is not known to you, but we bring you his greetings.'

His father was alive? Joseph swallowed hard.

'We hear that you are a wise and fair-minded man,' said Judah, completely unaware that he had once called this respected ruler all the names under the sun. 'May we trade with you?'

Joseph's tongue seemed to be stuck to the roof of his mouth. He could not utter a word.

'They may be foreigners, my lord,' whispered Kai, 'but it would be cruel to deny them, wouldn't you say?'

Joseph staggered to his feet. He pressed his fingertips on to the table to still their trembling. 'Where is the rest of your family?' he asked, praying that his sweet little brother, Benjamin, was still alive.

Joseph's brothers entered the room.

'Our father is at home and our brothers are all here,' said Reuben.

'All?'

'Save one, my lord. Benjamin. He has remained behind to look after our father.'

'There are no others?'

'None, my lord. Except one who died.'

'Died?' echoed Joseph, incredulously.

'Yes,' returned Judah. 'He was killed by a mountain lion.'

Rage welled up in Joseph's heart. Was that what they had told his father? Was that why Jacob had not come searching for his lost son?

'Liars!' bellowed Joseph. 'Throw them in prison!'

'My lord, what for?' cried Kai, who had never seen his master treat anyone like this before.

'Have we offended you, my lord?' asked Judah.

'Offended me?' echoed Joseph. 'Yes! You have offended me!' Then, catching sight of Kai's worried face he said, 'You... you are spies – come to see if we are broken by the famine.'

'My lord, this is untrue!' protested Reuben.

'Take them out of my sight!' Joseph cried, putting his hands to his face to conceal his emotion. 'Wait,' he mumbled. 'Wait one moment.'

His anger was fading. He did not really want to see his brothers imprisoned. No. What he really wanted was to see his father and Benjamin again. He dropped his hands to his sides.

'You...you say you are not spies. I wish you to prove it. Bring me the missing Canaanite brother, the one you left behind. In the meantime, one of you will remain as hostage.'

Nine bewildered and frightened brothers set off for home, leaving one behind. When they told their father what had happened he was furious.

'Monsters!' he accused. 'That's what I have for sons! What kind of fool do you take me for? You have kept the money I gave you and traded Simeon for the grain, haven't you?'

'No, Father,' protested Reuben.

'Haven't you, Judah!' Jacob persisted, glaring at his hot-headed, impulsive son.

'Father, I know you mistrust me,' said Judah earnestly. 'And I wish I could make things right between us. But you have to believe me. Simeon is safe, but to ensure his release we must take Benjamin.'

Benjamin had grown into a courageous young man. He took Jacob's withered hand in his. 'Don't worry, Father,' he said. 'I can take care of myself.'

As they set off, Judah turned to his father. 'I have disappointed you over many years,' he admitted. 'But I swear to you, I will die rather than return without them both.'

When the brothers arrived, Joseph was dismayed to see that Jacob was not with them.

'Your father…. Is he still alive?'

'He's old and frail, my lord, but he is still alive.'

'And the missing brother, the one you promised to bring to me – which is he?'

A well-grown young man stepped forward. 'I am Benjamin, my lord.'

Joseph's eyes smarted. 'Benjamin!' he exclaimed hoarsely. 'How you have aged!'

Benjamin stared at him in surprise. 'Aged, my lord?'

'Er…I imagined you younger, is what I meant.'

When Simeon was brought to them, the brothers greeted one another with such delight that Joseph's stomach twisted with jealousy. These were not the young hot-heads who had once thrown him into a well and then sold him. These were

mature men, husbands and fathers, men whose sense of family loyalty had grown deeper with the years. How he wished he was one of them still.

'Eat and rest,' he said heavily, 'for tomorrow you have far to travel.'

The brothers were given a room in which to spend the night and were generously supplied with food and drink. While they were laughing together over their meal, Joseph paced up and down outside the door. 'I must find a reason to keep Benjamin here,' he muttered to himself. 'Then Father will come.'

'I am Benjamin, my lord.'

At last he saw how it could be done. He called Kai to him and explained his plan.

Later that evening, Joseph summoned his brothers. He held up a magnificent golden goblet, studded with jewels.

'From this priceless goblet,' he announced, 'given to me by Pharaoh himself, I drink to your good health.'

The brothers joined in the toast. Then Joseph handed the cup to Kai. 'Tomorrow,' he whispered, 'before they reach the hills....'

The following day the brothers set off for Canaan. But before they had travelled many miles, Kai and two guards came galloping up.

'Halt in the name of Pharaoh!' cried Kai. 'My Lord Zaphenath-paneah has shown you kindness and hospitality, and you insult him by stealing from his house! Empty your saddle-bags.'

The brothers looked at each other in bewilderment. Judah tried to refuse but the guards ignored him and emptied each saddle-bag in turn on to the ground. From Benjamin's bag tumbled the golden goblet.

Benjamin turned frantic eyes on his brothers as one of the guards stepped forward to arrest him.

The brothers were taken to Joseph's house and paraded in front of him like criminals.

'My lord,' pleaded Judah, 'you have asked for the life of the one who is responsible. To take Benjamin's life would be to break his father's heart. I ask, therefore, that you accept my life instead, as a ransom for his.'

There was a long silence.

In all his life Joseph had never been so moved. The love which had made Judah so jealous all those years ago had not

'Do you still not know who I am?' said Joseph.

diminished, nor had his impulsive nature changed. But oh, how courageous Judah seemed now, how loyal, how loving, standing there so straight and offering up his own life for the sake of an old, old man. Joseph looked at the anxious faces of his eleven brothers and love rose in his throat until it threatened to choke him.

'Leave us!' he ordered his servants. 'All of you, go!'

When the twelve sons of Jacob were alone in the room

Joseph went up to Judah. 'Do you still not know who I am, my brother?' he asked in a voice rough with unshed tears.

But Judah did not know.

Strangely, it was Benjamin – the only brother who did not know that Joseph might still be alive – who understood first. 'Joseph?' he whispered, hardly daring to believe.

The brothers raced back to Canaan with joy in their hearts. They tumbled over one another to tell their father the good news, to explain how it had all come about, how generous and forgiving Joseph was, how he wanted them all to move to Egypt, how he had sent wagons to make the journey easier.

Eagerly they made ready, packing up their possessions, loading up the carts, preparing their wives and children for the journey ahead.

Jacob hardly knew where to put himself; he was irritable and joyful by turns. 'Stay together!' he commanded from his seat on the first of the wagons. 'It's an important day tomorrow. I want you all there!'

'Do you think he'll ever die?' Judah said laughingly.

'I doubt it,' grinned Benjamin. 'But if he does, at least now he can go in peace.'

As they travelled across the desert Jacob gazed up at the soaring blue sky. 'I *know*,' he told God. 'I know I wasn't very forgiving. But for all those years he was lost to me. If it had been your son, wouldn't you have been aggrieved? But tomorrow I shall see my beloved Joseph, and for that I thank you from the depths of my soul.' He shook his head wryly. 'I shall also say,' he added, 'that I do not understand you sometimes.'

They stopped on the road some miles from the city. Jacob peered into the distance. A chariot was approaching, sending up

At last, Jacob was reunited with his son, Joseph.

clouds of dust. In the chariot was a man. Jacob's mouth parched.

The chariot came closer. Through the swirling dust Jacob recognized Joseph's dear face and let out a hoarse cry. Joseph sprang to the ground and sprinted the final yards. As they came together the two men began to cry. They held each other close and wept upon each other's neck. Tenderly they spoke the other's name.

And then Joseph took the old man in his arms and bore his father home.

MOSES

I n the darkness was the sound of a man running. Swift footsteps echoed softly, then stumbled. The man rolled to the ground, gulping air.

Torchlight flared through the streets of Memphis as soldiers searched for him. They smashed doors, hauled people from their beds, ripping through the Hebrew camp like a hurricane.

'Where is he?' A guard seized an old man.

'I've told you. I don't know.'

'Jog his memory!' sneered one of the soldiers. The butt end of a spear clubbed the old man to the ground.

The fugitive hid in the shadows as the soldiers stormed through the streets, thrusting flaming torches through windows, roaring, 'Where is he?' into the faces of the frightened Hebrews.

He darted into a forgotten alleyway, hurtled along winding streets, through open squares, beneath the vast statues of strange Egyptian gods – Anubis with his jackal-head, Horus with his sceptre. He zig-zagged between the columns of a temple, so tall it seemed to touch the cold stars. As he sped onwards his foot

Moses ran through the streets of Memphis, pursued by the Egyptian soldiers.

sent a pebble spinning across the flagstones, rattling out a warning to the soldiers. They turned towards the sound and gave chase. Soon there were hundreds of them running, screaming after him. The man threw himself around a corner.

Then a hand slapped over his mouth, hauling him roughly into a doorway.

'It's over,' he thought.

But the hand was gentle.

'Aaron?' He looked at his own brother with amazement. Aaron thrust the reins of a camel into his hands.

'Quickly, take the beast.'

'You're helping a murderer. Rameses will have you killed, too.'

'I'm helping my brother,' Aaron hissed. 'And if you would only go quickly, Rameses need never know. Now ride!'

As the man swung into the saddle a soldier howled, 'Moses!'

Aaron helped his brother, Moses, to flee the city of Memphis.

But he had gone. Galloping furiously, he fled past the Hall of Kings, past the vast, lonely pyramids, away from Egypt towards the dawn.

Rameses was furious. He stood on the balcony of his great palace, his gold crown gleaming red in the evening sun. Before him, in the shifting haze, lay the desert that had swallowed Moses. There was no point in searching any longer. They would never find him out there now.

'I was too merciful, Menephtah,' he told his son. 'I allowed this Hebrew to betray my trust. Beware of such weakness when it is your turn to rule.'

From the cold glint in his father's eye, Menephtah understood that he must forget Moses now. Although they had been raised together in the palace as brothers, Moses was now no more than the child of a Hebrew slave.

'A pharaoh must be just,' he reminded his father, uneasily.

Rameses warned his son, Menephtah, about the dangers of being a weak pharaoh.

In the desert
Moses met Jethro,
the leader of the
Midianite people.

'To Egyptians, yes!' Rameses spat the words out like snake
venom. 'But for Hebrews the price of disobedience is death.'

Then he signalled the guards below to plunge their swords
into the shackled bodies of a group of Hebrew slaves.

'I will make the Nile flow red with their blood,' Rameses
snarled.

Far away, in the land of Midian, the bleached desert landscape gave way at last to dusty rocks and jagged mountains. Tufts of coarse grass clung to the craggy boulders. In a sheltered hollow stood a cluster of Midianite tents.

The Midianite leader stared curiously at the man on the camel. He stepped forward to greet Moses, then ordered food and wine to be spread before them.

'My name is Jethro,' he said. 'These tents, these sheep, are my city.'

Moses shrugged, showing the palms of his hands. 'I possess nothing,' he said.

Jethro frowned. He stared at Moses' soft hands, at the fine quality of the robe spread out around him on the ground, and at the camel. Moses did not look poor to him.

'Your clothes...?' Jethro protested.

'Egyptian, yes. But I have no nation. I was conceived in slavery.' Moses clenched his fists. 'And born in the stench of death.'

The Midianite sensed that the stranger had a story to tell. He studied Moses inquisitively, his face intent.

'I will tell you everything,' Moses said, watching as Jethro helped himself to food. 'And then you can tell me what you think....'

And so Jethro heard about the Hebrews, a whole race put to slavery, forced to make bricks for the cities and pyramids of Rameses, whipped until they cried out, whipped until they died. But he learned, too, how determined the Hebrews had been to survive, how for every man who died, two were born.

And then Moses told Jethro about the murder of the Hebrew children.

Jethro heard how the last-born boy from each Hebrew family was snatched at sword-point by Egyptian soldiers – even at the

moment of birth; how they were bundled into sacks, loaded into carts, dropped into the suffocating waters of the Nile like worthless stones.

The Midianite stared, open-mouthed. A gust of wind swirled dust into the air and brought tears to his eyes.

In the hot, shimmering air Moses imagined those faraway children coming back to life, miraculously grown into men now, wading out of the river, wresting swords from the hands of Pharaoh's men, forcing the soldiers into the water, watching them drown.

'But why?' Jethro asked, rousing Moses from his dream. 'What harm could those babies have done?'

'They would have grown into men,' Moses explained. 'Men who might have refused to be slaves any longer, who might have risen up and made war with Rameses. He was afraid.'

Then Moses told the Midianite leader how, as a baby, he alone of the last-born had survived the slaughter.

After his birth his mother had kept him hidden until his cries threatened to give him away. She made a little ark, woven from bullrushes, and when she was sure it would float she put her baby in it and set him free upon the river. Miriam, her daughter, hid amongst the reeds to watch. She saw her brother drift down the Nile – straight into the arms of the Pharaoh's daughter.

Miriam was frightened at first, but when the Egyptian princess smiled at the tiny baby and the baby smiled back, Miriam knew that her brother was safe. The wealthy young woman cuddled the Hebrew boy and told her friends she was going to keep him.

'He'll need milk,' Miriam said, drawing near. 'I know a woman who can feed him for you.... Shall I fetch her?'

And so Moses' mother became her own son's nurse.

'I was a cuckoo', said Moses, 'floating into Egypt's nest.'

Moses grew up singing the stories of the Hebrews in the palaces of Egypt. Eventually he was sent with Rameses' son, Menephtah, to the great libraries of Heliopolis to study under learned teachers. Moses was happy in Heliopolis. There he was neither Egyptian nor Hebrew, just himself.

But when the two young men returned to Memphis Moses heard once more the wailing of Hebrew slaves.

'Everywhere I went, I could hear them,' he said. 'And suddenly their cries became my cries, their pain, my pain.

'One day I was driving in my chariot past the quarry where they worked. The sun was blazing down. I saw my own people without water to drink, without rest. As I went on I came to a hidden place. There was an Egyptian there, raising his whip to one of the slaves. He lashed the man's back till blood ran. On and on. He wouldn't stop.' Moses was silent for a moment, then he said, 'I picked up a spade and I used it to kill him. And later, when Rameses found out, I ran away.'

The Midianite looked at the young man with compassion. 'Whatever you think you've lost,' said Jethro quietly, 'you'll find it in the desert.'

'Will I?'

'Go out there tomorrow with our sheep. You'll see that I am right.'

Many years passed. The desert closed around Moses and altered him beyond recognition. In Midianite clothing he tended Midianite sheep. He almost forgot the man he had once been.

But his brother Aaron had not forgotten him, although he too had changed, aged by long years of slavery and exhausted by the dangers of his life. Indeed, shortly after the death of Rameses, the old Pharaoh, Aaron was almost killed by a rock-fall.

'We had to move the stones for Menephtah's coronation procession,' he explained to his sister as she tore a strip from the hem of her skirt for a bandage. 'One man was buried by them.'

Miriam let out a weary sigh. 'Just another death.' She took her brother's hand and rubbed ointment into the wound. 'The first for our new Pharaoh.'

'To think he was a friend of Moses once.'

'Moses?' Miriam pulled a scornful face. 'That Egyptian?'

But Aaron's eyes had grown wistful. 'I dream about him sometimes.'

'Dreams!' Miriam wound the bandage tightly around his palm. 'When will our people open their eyes?'

Moses scrambled up a lonely track, following a stray sheep. The animal led him high on to the silent mountain. Out of the corner of his eye he saw a bush burst into flames, but paid it no heed. It was nothing, the sun burnt everything in this place. It was only when the wall of rock behind him blazed with light, a light more intense, more piercing than any sunlight, that Moses froze in his tracks and looked around him.

Fear leapt in his throat.

Flames were roaring from the bush, as white as molten iron – but within the eerie furnace the bush was still green.

And somewhere in this lonely place someone was calling his name.

Terrified, he tried to see past the fire but the light blinded him.

'Moses....'

'I...I am here....'

The air was swirling around him, whipping the words from his mouth and hurling them into the flames.

'Take off your sandals. You stand on holy ground.'

The voice was huge...vast, coming from everywhere, carried on the seething air. Moses fell to his knees. With trembling hands he fumbled with his sandals, desperate to obey.

'Moses....'

'Who is speaking? Who are you?'

'I am your God.'

Moses buried his face in his arms.

'I am the God of Abraham, of Isaac, of Jacob.'

Moses almost cried out with dread.

'Do you think I have not watched the sufferings of my people the Israelites in Egypt?' The fire darkened with rage, flared purple like welts on raw flesh. 'Now the suffering will end. I am sending you to bring them home to a land that flows

Moses stared in terror at the burning bush.

with milk and honey.'

Moses shook his head.

'I shall be with you,' God said.

'The Hebrews….' Moses stuttered. 'They will look for proof. They will ask me your name.'

The flames roared dangerously. 'I am who I am,' echoed the voice. 'Tell them the Lord God has sent you.'

Moses hung his head. He had to do what God commanded, yet how could he? He was a shepherd. He could not be a leader of men.

'I will give you signs,' said God. 'They will believe. Go with your brother Aaron. He will be your mouthpiece, and the Lord God your inspiration.'

And so Moses began the long walk back across the desert. Along the way he met Aaron, sent by God to welcome him. After a joyful reunion, the two brothers set off together for Memphis, inspired by God's message and determined to set their people free.

Moses had been right. The Hebrews would not believe him, even when he threw his staff on the ground and the Lord God gave a sign by changing it into a snake.

'I'm not following a man who's half-Egyptian,' muttered one of the elders to a great murmuring of agreement.

Then one man stood up and said, 'Listen! For years we wait, we pray for the moment. Now it comes and we argue. Let him at least try.'

So Moses and Aaron walked to the palace to seek an audience with Pharaoh, past the stone gods of Egypt, past the towering columns and high gates.

'The Lord God is merciful,' Aaron comforted his brother.

Moses shuddered. 'Merciful? I have felt the Lord God on my

flesh and He fills me with more fear than the King of Egypt.'
He handed his staff to Aaron. 'Today you will speak His words.'

When the two rough, bearded men arrived in the great hall,
Menephtah looked scathingly at them. He did not recognize
Moses from those faraway days.

'A petition from the Hebrew slaves?' Menephtah drawled.

'From the God of the Hebrews,' Aaron corrected.

Menephtah rolled his eyes. Did not these Hebrews know that
he, Pharaoh, was god in Egypt?

'Our God says,' continued Aaron, '"Let My people go."'

Menephtah turned to his courtiers and laughed.

'Or...' warned Aaron, 'the Lord God promises plagues upon
you and your people.'

'I shall be the one to devise punishments,' sneered the King.

Moses and
Aaron came to
the palace to
seek an audience
with Pharaoh.

'Though I can't promise plagues.' He stuck his tongue in his cheek. 'We lesser gods must do what we can.'

The Egyptians continued to mock, even when Aaron threw his staff to the ground and it reared up as a snake. The royal magicians were sent for, and they conjured up snakes from under their cloaks. And when the snake of the Hebrews consumed the Egyptian snakes, and then flew back into Aaron's hand as a staff, they still jeered.

'You will believe in God's power when the Lord God turns your god, the Nile, to blood,' said Aaron.

But the only response Menephtah made was to send out instructions for the Hebrews to work even harder.

The following day was the festival of the Nile. In great splendour the Egyptians came to worship their great river, the Hebrews to watch.

'Hail to thee, O Nile that comes to keep Egypt alive,' Menephtah intoned as the celebrations commenced.

As the words came from his mouth Moses struck the river with his staff.

The high priests of Egypt handed Pharaoh the ritual cup of river-water to drink, but as he put it to his lips the cheers of his people turned to screams. The waters of the Nile were foaming and belching. No longer were they clear and sparkling, but as red and as thick as blood.

And the water in Menephtah's mouth, the water which dribbled from his lips and dripped on to his white robe, it also had turned to blood.

For seven days all the water in Egypt thickened to blood and crawled under Egypt's sun.

Moses and Aaron went back to the palace, convinced that now Pharaoh would let their people go.

Menephtah stroked his son's hair and shrugged. 'This man tried to frighten us,' he crooned to the boy. 'But it was only a trick.'

'It was no trick,' said Moses. 'It was our God commanding.'

The King reached out and touched a statue of the goddess Heket, in the image of a frog. 'So *many* gods,' he taunted.

Aaron also put out his hand to the statue. He sent it crashing to the floor. Frogs poured out of the base until the palace was alive with them.

As the days passed, frogs filled the houses of Egypt, filled the bedchambers, the ovens, the kneading bowls.

'Will you let my people go?' Moses asked.

But Pharaoh would not let the Hebrews go.

Next the cattle and horses, the herds and flocks of the Egyptians, sickened and died, but the animals belonging to the Hebrews flourished.

A plague of frogs filled the houses of Egypt.

Still Menephtah would not let them go.

One by one, more plagues came.

The pyramids turned white with frost, hail flattened the crops, lightning shattered every tree.

'Pharaoh,' cried Moses. 'Let my people go!'

'No!' roared Menephtah. 'Let them stay and suffer.'

'Locusts will come upon the land,' warned Moses. 'And eat every plant….'

But Menephtah only laughed.

When the locusts had stripped bare every green thing that grew in Egypt and Pharaoh would still not set the Hebrews free, Moses stretched out his hand and for three days thick darkness came over the land of Egypt.

Menephtah turned his eyes up to the sky. 'Why is the sun-god powerless?' he demanded.

Moses knew that the next plague would tear at the Pharaoh's heart, just as it would tear at the heart of every family in the land. He begged Menephtah not to bring it upon his people.

'Gather your own life around you,' he pleaded. 'You have a son….'

'No!' bellowed Menephtah. 'You will not touch him!'

'Yes. Your child, and the first-born of all your people.' Moses warned. 'The Lord God chooses life. Choose with him now. Let my people go.'

The darkness deepened as Moses waited for Pharaoh's reply. Anger rose inside him. Surely Menephtah must believe in the Lord God by now? Surely he would not sacrifice his beloved child, and the first-born of all his subjects, rather than let the Hebrews go? But though Moses waited for a long time, Menephtah did not speak.

It was time to get ready. Moses moved among the houses in the Hebrew quarter, telling them what to do. First they must kill a lamb and smear its blood above the doors to their houses so that God would know them and would pass over them.

Then they must roast the lamb whole, and quickly prepare some unleavened bread to eat with it. While the food was cooking, the people must dress warmly for a journey, then eat as fast as they could manage. Everything must be ready by midnight. Because at midnight the angel of death would come.

There was no mistaking its presence. It surged through streets and up stairs, around corners and along passages. It moved faster than light, visiting every house in the twinkling of an eye. It came to grown men who were elder brothers, it came to children curled up on their pillows, to babies asleep in their mothers' arms. Relentless, indiscriminate, it took the life of every first-born in Egypt and left their bodies as empty shells.

And it came, of course, to Menephtah's son. The man who

Moses told the Hebrews what to do, so that the angel of death would pass over their houses.

had thought he was god fell down on his knees and wept like a child. He touched the boy's lifeless face, squeezed the child's limp hand, then, wild with grief, gathered his son's body in his arms and staggered through the great rooms of his palace, crying out as he ran, 'Let them GO! Let them take their God with them and GO!'

The Hebrews surged out of Memphis in their thousands, like a river that has broken its dam. They coursed into the wilderness with the wind in their eyes, an entire nation searching for the promised land.

Death came to Menephtah's son.

The Hebrews surged out of Egypt, guided by a great pillar of fire.

Miriam hugged a child in her arms as she ran. 'How do we know where to go?' the boy asked. And then his mouth opened in wonder as a great pillar of fire and smoke rose up in the desert to guide them.

As the Hebrews crossed the desert, Pharaoh grieved.

'Everything I love...' he sighed. 'Why can I keep nothing? I even had a friend among the Hebrews once. Gone. He would have dealt with those two sorcerers.'

The priest who was with him frowned. 'Don't you know their names?'

'I didn't ask.' Menephtah shrugged. 'They were slaves.'

'They were Aaron of the tribe of Levi. And his brother, Moses.'

The blood froze in Menephtah's veins. Moses? The man who had once been his brother? Oh, he would take his revenge on

Moses for this!

On and on across the endless desert travelled the Hebrews, until they reached the edge of the Red Sea. Where was this land Moses had promised? There was not even fresh water in this place, let alone milk and honey! Worn down, weary, they began to despair.

And then a small boy came running amongst them, shouting at the top of his voice.

'Moses!' he gasped. 'I saw…a cloud of dust… and then I saw chariots…horsemen…the sun glinting on armour.'

Moses groaned. Why could Menephtah not let them go? He called the Hebrews to the edge of the water.

'Save us, Moses,' begged his sister, Miriam.

'If you want to be saved, then stand and wait.'

The Hebrews uttered cries of disbelief. Stand and wait? With the thunder of hooves and the flash of spears growing closer by the minute? But what else could they do? A chill wind came off the sea.

Chariot wheels threw up clouds of sand, flags streamed in the air, swords

Filled with rage, Menephtah led his horsemen in pursuit of the fleeing Hebrews.

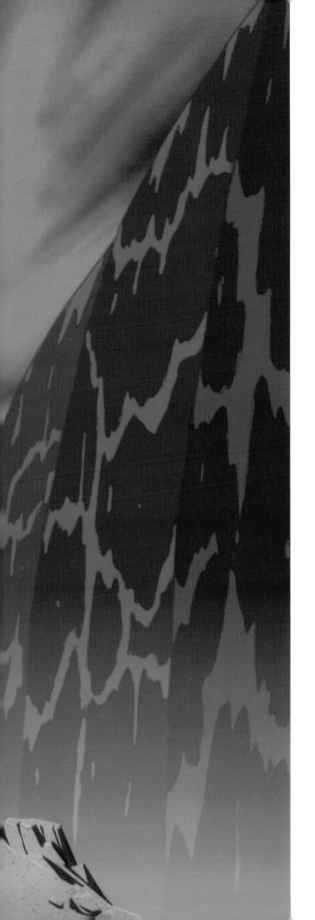

slashed the sunlight, ready for attack.

Behind the Hebrews, the wind began to howl. It tore at their clothes, screamed in their ears, whipped the sea into a roaring frenzy. And then Moses raised his staff.

Before their eyes the water reared up and parted. Bordered by two heaving, glassy walls of snarling water was a narrow path through the sea.

'Now!' commanded Moses. 'Cross!'

But no one dared. Trapped between two terrors, they could not move. Until a tiny child dropped his toy into the channel and ran to retrieve it. The great cliffs of water shivered but they did not fall.

The people watched for a brief second, and then, their hearts lifting, the entire Hebrew nation began to swarm through the cleft in the sea.

Behind them came Pharaoh's men. Terrified horses were lashed into obedience, chariot wheels span in the mud as the great Egyptian army plunged after them into the extraordinary breach.

But as the last Hebrew hurtled through, the waters merged behind him. And with an almighty roar, the sea crashed down over Menephtah's men.

Moses led the Hebrews through the parted waters to safety.

Safe on the other side, the Hebrews watched the soldiers drown. When the last petrified face had sunk beneath the waves, Moses shaded his eyes and looked sorrowfully at the far shore. From amid the tattered remains of his army, Menephtah stared back.

Miriam touched Moses' sleeve. 'Don't look back....' she said, gently. 'Nothing can stop us getting to the promised land now. Come and listen to your people singing to the Lord God. Join with us and rejoice.'

DAVID AND SAUL

S amuel was furious.

He cast a contemptuous eye over the huddle of soldiers and animals that had been captured from the Philistines, and then glared at Saul, still in his battle armour. The Lord God had told King Saul to destroy *everything* belonging to the enemy.

'Er…we captured the animals only for sacrifice,' Saul mumbled.

'Obedience to the Lord God is more important than mere sacrifice,' retorted the prophet Samuel. 'You have halted here and built a monument to yourself!'

Saul fumbled for more excuses, but the cold anger in Samuel's eye froze his tongue. Shame began to creep in Saul's blood. 'I have sinned,' he confessed. He fell to his knees. 'The

The prophet Samuel was furious with King Saul for building a monument to himself.

people wanted plunder. I shouldn't have listened to them. Forgive me....'

But Samuel shook his head. This was not the first time that Saul had disobeyed God.

God had chosen Saul to be the first King of Israel because the Israelites had demanded a king to lead them in battle, despite having been warned that kings – unlike God Himself – might lead them astray.

Until now, God had told Saul what to do. But Saul's disobedience meant that God could no longer rule through him. From now on, Saul must choose his own path – and the Israelites must follow.

'You have rejected the word of the Lord God,' Samuel said coldly. 'And now the Lord God rejects you.'

Saul froze. Rejected by God? No. It could not be true!

Samuel looked down on the cowering King. 'Today the Lord has torn the kingdom of Israel out of your hands.'

Saul cried out in horror.

'He will pass it on to another man. A better man than you.'

'Another man...?' The blood roared in Saul's ears.

'We shall not meet again,' muttered Samuel scornfully. 'Not to your dying day.'

Another man...a better man than you....

Day in, day out, the words echoed in Saul's head. They came to him in his sleep, so that he awoke trembling. They blurred the edges of his vision, dulled his hearing, and twisted his emotions so that dark thoughts spiralled endlessly to the surface.

He called upon God – but heard only silence.

One day, when he was sitting in his throne room, the nagging words came to him again.

'You shall not...' he raged between clenched teeth. 'I am

Everyday, Saul slipped further into madness.

king, I am....' He scrambled to his feet and swayed towards the watching courtiers. 'Do you hear?' he spat the words into their faces. 'This is the House of Saul! Saul is king in Israel.'

His son Jonathan forced his way through the crowded throne room.

'Father?' he murmured, approaching Saul gently. 'Father, how can I help you?'

Saul turned clouded eyes on his son. 'They're plotting and whispering,' he accused. 'They say they want a new king. They've turned against us, Jonathan.'

Jonathan nodded uneasily. Ironically, his father was right. The courtiers thought this madness was punishment from the Lord God, and although Saul had ruled wisely, now they wanted him gone.

Jonathan's sister, Michal, hurried over. 'Tell us what is troubling you,' she begged her father.

But Saul shook his head. He slumped on his throne and buried his face in his hands.

'Shall we send for the Holy Prophet, Samuel?' Michal suggested.

'No! Not him!' cried Saul in terror. 'Not Samuel! Never!'

He began to shake with fear as the words swam in his head. *Another man. A better man than you....* No. Not Samuel... never....

Abner, the commander of the Israelite army, was concerned for the bewildered brother and sister.

'I've seen men suffer like this before,' he said softly. 'It is an evil spirit. I have known music calm them, give peace to the spirit.'

'Then find someone,' returned Jonathan desperately. 'Find someone to help him!'

'My lord, I have heard of a boy, David, one of the sons of Jesse in Bethlehem. He plays beautifully, they say....'

'Then send for him.'

David was out alone, tending his father's sheep, when he heard a noise. When he turned to look, his heart stood still.

Behind him was a great, snarling bear, so close that he could smell the stench of its breath.

Slowly, David slipped a pebble into his sling. Keeping his eye on the bear, he swung the sling behind him and loosed the pebble straight at the head of the great beast. The stone hit the creature between the eyes. He heard the crunch of shattering bone. The bear fell to the ground, dead.

'David!'

David was astonished to see his father struggling up the

opposite slope towards him.

'Did you see?' the boy cried. His pulse was still racing and his voice shook a little. 'There was a bear attacking the sheep....'

'Never mind that now. Do you have your harp with you?'

'Yes.'

'You have everything you need then.' Jesse took a deep breath. 'You have been summoned to court, David. To King Saul's palace in Gibeah.'

'*Me?*'

'To play your songs to King Saul.'

David frowned. Why on earth did King Saul want him at the palace? 'Is this...is this why the prophet Samuel visited us? Is

When David turned round, he was confronted by a great, snarling bear.

this why he asked to see me?'

A year ago, the prophet Samuel had come to Jesse's house and had demanded to see all of his eight sons. And when David had appeared, the youngest and therefore the last, Samuel had smiled a smile of recognition and had said, 'This is the choice of the Lord God.'

Was this what he had been chosen for?

But Jesse only shrugged awkwardly. 'Don't you worry about that now. I told you we wouldn't talk about that.' He handed David some bread and a wineskin. 'Just keep safe,' he urged lovingly.

David played his harp to soothe the troubled Saul.

Abner had been right. Music did indeed soothe Saul. All year long, whenever the King grew agitated, whenever he fell into despair or was roused to a frenzy, David was sent for to calm him.

And then one night, as David was playing Saul to sleep, Abner and Jonathan burst into the room.

'There is news, Father,' said Jonathan breathlessly. 'Our scouts have sighted the Philistine army.'

Saul sat up, very straight. 'Tell me where,' he commanded. Suddenly he was calm and in control. The Lord God had chosen him to defend the Hebrews against their enemies. He would not fail his God this time.

David had never before seen armies massed for war. The Israelites, lined up on one side of the valley, looked dangerous enough, but the Philistine army, ranked on the far side, looked even more impressive.

David wove his way through the soldiers until he found his own brothers.

'The fighting is about to start,' hissed Eliab, the eldest. 'Get back to your sheep.'

'Israelites!' came a booming voice. 'Listen to me!'

'I'm the King's shield bearer,' David protested. 'I'm entitled to —'

All eyes turned to the Philistines. Someone had stepped out from their ranks. He was a great ox of a man, twice the size of any of David's brothers, a huge, fearsome warrior, a battlehorse in human guise.

'Choose someone!' the giant bellowed. 'Send him out to fight me!'

The Hebrews exchanged nervous glances. No one moved.

'Send your God if you want,' Goliath jeered.

Rumours of Goliath's stature had reached the Hebrews, but no one had believed them until now.

David was puzzled. 'Isn't anyone going out there to fight him?' he asked.

'I told you,' muttered Eliab, 'get back behind the line.'

'He has insulted our Lord God,' returned David hotly. 'Our people.'

'Didn't you hear me?' hissed Eliab. He grabbed his little brother and thrust him away.

'Someone should fight him,' grumbled David as he made his way back to the King. 'The Lord God must have anointed someone for this task. Chosen someone specially.'

And then his stomach lurched with excitement, because the Lord God had indeed chosen someone…he had chosen David! Surely this was the task for which God had singled him out. This was what Samuel had meant!

David ran up to Saul. 'I will fight Goliath for you!' he announced confidently.

Saul and his officers chuckled.

'In the hilltops above Bethlehem I've killed lions. I've killed a bear!'

Jonathan studied David. 'Goliath is no worse,' he conceded.

'And the Lord God will protect me.' David pleaded.

Saul looked coldly at his cowardly officers. None of them had volunteered. Let them see how they felt when a boy stood in their place. 'Give the boy my armour,' he said.

David approached the huge man, Goliath.

But the armour was far too heavy, so without it, David walked over to a nearby brook and selected five small pebbles. Then, head held high, he marched towards Goliath.

As the boy drew closer, the warrior seemed to grow even bigger. David's heart pounded but he kept on going.

'What am I? A dog?' growled Goliath. 'You send out a boy to chase me!'

David swallowed hard. 'You have defied the army of the Lord God,' he called back. 'I have come to fight you in His name.'

David's brothers could not bear to look.

'You've come to be food for the vultures,' Goliath taunted, weighing his spear in his hand.

David slipped a pebble into his sling with trembling fingers.

As Goliath shouldered his spear and took aim, David let fly the pebble. Just like the bear, Goliath crumpled to the ground, dead.

The shocked Philistines turned on their heels and fled. If a boy could slay their champion with a blow, think what the rest might do!

As the Israelites howled with delight, David dropped to his knees in front of Saul, but the King's son, Jonathan, indignantly pulled David back to his feet. This boy was their saviour – he should be raised shoulder high! Overwhelmed with admiration, the crown prince of Israel embraced the shepherd boy from Bethlehem.

Saul, too, was overjoyed. The boy had proved to be a better man than all his captains and soldiers put together! But as Saul watched Jonathan give David his own sword and cloak, the words began to crawl up the inside of his skull. *Another man*, they whispered. *A better man than you....*

David swung the pebble and let it fly.

David and
Jonathan
returned from
war, victorious.

Saul's joy turned sour and seeped away.

David grew to manhood at Saul's court. Within four years, he had risen to the rank of captain in Saul's army, serving Saul's people, defending Saul's borders.

But while David was away with the troops, Saul's thoughts were left unguarded. The words grew louder in his head, David's face loomed larger in his mind's eye – and there was no music to send them away.

So Saul set up court outdoors beneath a tamarisk tree. He thought the birdsong might prove soothing.

When David returned to Gibeah, victorious in battle, his gaze was drawn to Saul's daughter, Michal. She looked back shyly, her cheeks flushed, her eyes bright.

Saul observed the attraction between them, and smiled to himself. He planned to set a trap for David, with Michal as bait.

Encouraged by Jonathan, David asked Saul for Michal's hand in marriage, although he did not expect the King to give his consent – Michal was a princess while David was a poor man.

But, to David's surprise, the King readily agreed, although in truth Saul had no intention of letting David into his family. Once married to Michal, David would be a prince, and as a prince he would be a contender for the throne.

Cunningly, Saul suggested that the wedding should take place only after David had defeated the Philistines who were invading the north of the kingdom in great numbers. Saul allowed David to take only a few hundred men with him. It was obvious to Saul that David would be so badly outnumbered by the Philistines that his death would be inevitable.

'You will defeat them, David,' Saul said confidently. 'And *then* the wedding,' he added, certain that the promise could never be kept.

Not suspecting a trap, David set off willingly. He was determined to win the battle and marry Michal. And although he was indeed outnumbered, after praying to God for help, he and his troops defeated the Philistines. Now Saul had no choice but to let the wedding take place.

As David rode to his wedding the streets were full of cheering people.

'Saul has laid low thousands!' they cried. 'But David has slain ten thousand!'

David dismounted and smiled at the crowd. Then, with eyes and heart full of love, he walked towards his bride.

As David took Michal's hand, Saul watched. The words were louder than ever. *Another man*, they drummed. *David has slain ten thousands....*

Saul stared at David with hatred in his eyes.

Jonathan touched his father's arm. 'The lord King should not despise his servant David,' he whispered. 'We should cherish him, not fear him.'

'Forgive me, Jonathan,' Saul sounded flustered. 'I was wrong. I swear by the Lord God never to harm David. I love him like my own son.'

But the words continued

Michal and David fell in love.

to hammer at his brain, even as David took Michal for his wife.

Saul needed David's music more than ever now. Night after night, David sat with him playing his harp.

But the words would not go away.

One night, Saul could bear it no longer. He leapt out of bed and snatched up his spear. David stumbled to his feet, wide-eyed.

Saul heaved back the spear and flung it with all his might at David. The blade caught the harp and split it in two before lodging in the wall. Saul fell upon the shaft and wrenched it free.

David's heart thundered as he backed away from his king. He had seen Saul in many moods, but he had never known him violent before. Then David saw hatred flaring in the King's eyes and he understood that this was more than a passing mood. Saul wanted him dead, and he wanted it with a ferocity that chilled the blood. David's hand went to his dagger – but he found he could not hurt God's chosen king, not even to save his own life.

In a mad fury Saul flung his spear at David.

Instead he ran away, hurtling along the corridors of the palace to his own room.

'Guards!' yelled Saul. 'Close the palace! Lock all the doors!'

Michal helped David escape through the window. Then she heaved a huge clay pot into their bed and threw the covers over it. When Saul's guards came hammering at the door she demanded, 'Would you enter the room of a sick man?'

The strategy bought a little time. Precious minutes passed before Saul himself arrived and kicked the silent figure beneath the bedclothes.

The pot shattered into a thousand pieces.

'You have conspired with your father's enemies!' Saul snarled. 'We shall have to find you a new husband.'

A new husband? The dismay on Michal's face told Saul that David had now turned his own child against him…. Rage thickened in his throat.

Soldiers were sent out into the countryside to search by torchlight.

Jonathan was bewildered by the turn of events. He loved his father, but he loved David too. That night

he could not sleep. He paced the corridors of the palace, and finally, just before dawn, went outdoors.

David, who was hiding, saw him and called out softly.

'David!' Jonathan exclaimed.

'Is it safe?'

Jonathan nodded. He came near to David and laid his hand on his shoulder.

'I will have to leave,' David said unhappily. 'Make my life in the hills.'

'Go safely,' whispered Jonathan with tears in his eyes.

Saul spent the following day beneath the tamarisk tree, ranting.

Jonathan could not bear to see his father hurt and damaged like this, but nor could he tolerate hearing David abused.

'He has run off like a dog,' Saul sneered, 'after he tried to kill me.'

His courtiers nodded wearily.

Saul ranted at his courtiers under the tamarisk tree.

'That is a lie, Father,' retorted Jonathan, white-lipped with anger.

'Silence! You're no son of mine!' Saul turned accusingly to his courtiers. 'Why did no one tell me these two were plotting together?'

'David would never raise a hand against you,' Jonathan muttered, turning his back on his father and walking away.

'If David becomes king,' Saul called out after him, 'then he will have to destroy the house of Saul – and you with it.'

Jonathan strode off with his head held high, although inside he felt raw. Why did his father make him choose between them? Would he ever be able to love brother and father equally again?

Saul began stirring up his courtiers against David with renewed vigour. He reminded them that they were of the tribe of Benjamin while David was of the tribe of Judah. Tribal loyalty was at stake.

At last he had their interest. 'My lord, we will hunt him down,' they agreed. 'Wherever he is, he must be found.'

'Throughout my kingdom, David is henceforth an outlaw,' Saul pronouced in triumph.

But before they could begin their search, a messenger arrived.

'I have news,' he said breathlessly.

'Well?'

'The Holy Prophet, Samuel, is dead.'

Saul's eyes lit up. 'So we shall never meet again...?' But then he frowned. There were people who claimed to be able to speak to the dead. 'Let it be decreed,' he said, 'that it shall be a capital crime to call up spirits of the dead.' He rubbed his hands together gleefully. 'Now, let's run this boy to earth!'

But they did not run David to earth. His years as a shepherd served him well. He knew the countryside inside out. He made his home in hill caves, far away from the palace – and he was not alone. Many people fled from Saul's rage and joined David in hiding. Without David to soothe him, the King was becoming increasingly irrational.

Saul scoured the countryside for months, travelling further and further in his search, telling everyone who crossed his path that David must die.

David and Abishai entered Saul's camp by night.

One night, by chance, he camped close to David's hideaway.

David's scouts brought him word of Saul's encampment. David hesitated. Should he go now, or should he wait until Saul slept? In the dead of night, David and his captain, Abishai, went to investigate. They found Abner, Saul's commander, asleep in the doorway of Saul's tent. They stepped over him and entered.

David looked down on Saul's face. Even in sleep the poor man looked troubled and fearful. Abishai drew his sword and raised it, but David grasped his wrist to prevent him from bringing it crashing down.

'We cannot strike the Lord's anointed, Abishai,' he said softly. Then he took Saul's spear and left.

When morning came, David stood on the hillside overlooking the camp and held the spear aloft.

'My lord Abner,' he called. 'Is this how you protect your king?'

Abner looked up in amazement.

And so did Saul. 'Is that you, David, my son?' he cried excitedly. 'Oh, David....' Saul's voice caught in his throat. 'David....'

'Why do you hunt me, my lord?'

Suddenly Saul missed David more than words could say. 'Come back to me,' he begged.

Slowly David shook his head. 'Do not let me die on this foreign soil, my lord, hunted down like an animal.'

'I will never harm you again, David,' promised Saul earnestly. 'Come back!'

David's heart was like lead. He remembered the rush of air as Saul's spear had hurtled towards him, remembered the fury in Saul's eyes. Hatred like that could not be buried for ever. One day it would well up again.

David thrust the spear into the soil at his feet and walked

David held up Saul's spear and called down to the King.

away. But oh…if only Saul could always be like this….

Saul stood very still and watched David disappear. In that moment he knew that he loved David, but he knew also that the feeling would not last. Soon the words would come back to haunt him, the jealousy would return. His eyes stung.

'My lord King,' said a guard, coming close.

'Yes?'

'The Philistine army has broken through our defences. They are marching north in force.'

'Strike camp.' Saul blinked away his misery. He straightened his back. 'We must face the enemy.'

David also heard of the Philistine attack. But when he returned to his camp he heard worse news.

'Amalakite bandits, my lord. They have taken the women.'

David frowned. 'I will go after them. As soon as we return we will go in force to join King Saul.'

When Saul came in sight of the enemy at Gilboa he was shocked. There were thousands upon thousands of them.

He fell to his knees. 'Lord God, speak to me,' he pleaded. 'Tell me what I should do.'

But he knew as he spoke the words that there would be no answer.

He got to his feet and beckoned Abner close. 'I must seek counsel from the dead,' he murmured.

'But you have decreed —'

'Find someone!'

Abner thought carefully. 'There is a woman near here,' he revealed, 'at Endor.'

At the witching hour, in the very depths of the night, Saul, his cloak wrapped about his face as a disguise, was taken to the woman's cave. Before her was a hole in the floor from which smoke curled and twisted.

Although she knew that it was forbidden to summon spirits, she took Saul's gold. Then she took a handful of crystals and threw them into the hole. The smoke billowed and swirled about her and then surged upwards forming a glowing, cloudy pillar. She breathed deeply.

'What can you see?' demanded Saul.

'Wait,' she said dreamily. 'We must wait for my familiar spirit to arise.'

She looked into the mist, but then she seemed to shrink back. 'It is not my familiar.' Indeed, she had only ever pretended to see spirits, but now there really *was* one. Her voice shook with fear. 'It is an old man. He is —' And then she cried

In the cave of Endor, Saul saw the spirit of the prophet Samuel.

out in dread.

'Why has my rest been disturbed?' demanded a voice.

'Who is that?' Saul could see nothing.

'It is the Holy Prophet, Samuel,' whispered the witch, peering into the smoke.

'Why have I been summoned?' asked the spirit of Samuel.

'My lord, the Philistines have invaded the kingdom. The Lord God no longer answers my prayers,' explained Saul.

'You are the one who turned against the Lord God,' the voice reminded him curtly.

'I must have counsel.'

'The Lord God has torn the kingdom from you,' Samuel said coldly, 'and given it to David.'

'David....' Saul could hardly speak his name. 'David...will... be king? When?'

'Today. Today, when the sun is high in the sky, the Lord God will deliver you and your son to death. It is your dying day.'

There was a dreadful silence.

'I am not ready,' whispered the terrified King.

'If only you had listened,' reproached the fading voice, 'and obeyed.'

Drained and grief-stricken, Saul nonetheless made ready for battle with dignity. He would go to his death like a king.

As he and Jonathan prepared to lead the charge he said, 'In the name of the Lord God we fight the enemy today.'

'As you command, Father,' Jonathan replied.

Saul looked at his son for a long moment. 'Forgive me, Jonathan,' he pleaded. 'I have wronged you and I have wronged my son David.'

Jonathan's heart soared. His father's mind was clear, his father's heart was repentant. 'I forgive you, Father,' he said joyfully. Now he could love both men equally again!

And then his father gave the signal for the battle to begin.

David was on his way to join the fighting when he saw a lone horseman riding towards him. The man dismounted and fell to his knees in front of him.

'My lord David,' he said heavily, 'a battle has been fought, at Gilboa.'

'What news of King Saul? Of Jonathan, my brother.'

The man picked up a handful of dust and let it trickle through his fingers. David's heart seemed to stand still as he watched.

Saul was dead. And so was his dear brother, Jonathan.

David reached the abandoned battlefield as the sky turned red. It matched the bloodstained earth on which lay the thousand Israelite dead, their eyes blind to all sunsets for ever.

'In life, in death, they were not divided,' David breathed, coming upon the bodies of Saul and of Jonathan, side by side. 'They were swifter than eagles, stronger than lions. How are the mighty fallen....'

Saul and his son
Jonathan lay dead
on the battlefield.

Many years later King David returned to the battlefield at Gilboa. The air was full of birdsong, full of hope. The tribes of Israel were united under their new king. The Philistines had been defeated. A great city was being built at Jerusalem.

But still David did not forget.

JONAH

'I suppose it will have to do,' Jonah muttered grumpily, parting the branches with his bony fingers and peering in. 'Bit cooler, at any rate.'

It was certainly the most suitable shade he was likely to find. The leafy branches of the tree drooped to the ground creating a shady cavern, ideal for a person to sit and think, sheltered from the blazing sun. He crept in, plonked his scraggy frame on the ground and eased his shoulders against the knobbly trunk. He grunted irritably. The bark was scratchy. And some wretched insect was buzzing around outside…not to mention children's voices in the distance…. Well, they'd better not come buzzing round his tree, that was all!

Jonah found a cool place to sit under the shady branches of a tree.

Hundreds of miles away, in the city of Nineveh, the high priest of Ishtar was raising his hands to the great statue which soared high above the temple walls.

'Almighty, all-powerful Ishtar of Nineveh...' he intoned. 'Sublime mother-goddess....'

In front of the statue was an altar fire with shooting flames. Two beautiful temple-maidens danced a sinuous dance. The priest poured oil on the fire, creating impressive clouds of blue smoke. 'We give you thanks and praise, O glorious and terrible Ishtar,' he chanted, 'for the greatness of your majesty....'

A white dove watched from high above. As the smoke curled upwards, the bird spread its wings and flew away.

'Can't catch me!' yelled a small boy, hurtling in circles around Jonah's tree.

'Can!' retorted his sister, charging after him.

'Wait!' The boy skidded to a halt as he heard an infuriated huff come from inside the tree.

'Noise, noise, noise!' muttered Jonah angrily.

'Shh...Come here. Quick,' whispered the boy, parting the leaves and peeping in. 'It's Jonah!'

His sister tiptoed close and peered through the gap.

'I'm tired of this place,' Jonah grumbled, shaking his fist indignantly at thin air. 'Never any peace and quiet...scarcely hear yourself think! What a world....'

The children clapped their hands over their mouths to smother their giggles. Jonah spread his hands wide in despair. 'All I see around me is people disobeying God. Doing their own thing. Going their own way. No respect for God! And no respect for those who believe in Him.'

The girl nudged her brother. 'They call him Jonah the

moaner,' she whispered, shaking with laughter.

'Clear off!' snarled Jonah. Helpless with giggles the children staggered away. Jonah ground his teeth as he leant back against the trunk of the tree. Humph! Children would not have dared behave like that when he was a lad. The world was going from bad to worse. He yawned…. His eyelids began to droop.

The white dove wheeled in the air above the tree.

'Jonah!'

Jonah rubbed his eyes and groaned. Couldn't a man take forty winks without someone coming along?

'Jonah.'

'What now!' he burst out. Blasted kids! Right, he would show them! He scrambled to his feet and emerged from his shelter, shaking his fist.

'Jonah.'

He gazed around, baffled. That was not a child's voice, and anyway there was no one in sight….

'Who is it?' he demanded crossly.

The dove circled low above Jonah's head. 'Do I really have to tell you who I am?' asked the voice, sounding a little amused. 'Do I?'

Jonah frowned. How could a voice come out of thin air like that? It did not make sense. Unless…. 'O-oh…' Jonah's heart thundered. His mouth grew dry. 'What do you want with me, O Lord God?'

'I have chosen you to be my prophet.'

Jonah gulped. A prophet…? That was a heavy responsibility.

'What message am I to take to my people?' he asked doubtfully.

'The message is not for your people. It is for the people of Nineveh.'

'Nineveh?' echoed Jonah incredulously. Nineveh was a devilish place, everybody knew that! 'But Nineveh's miles away!' he complained. 'No…no! I'm sorry.…' He dived back into the tree to collect his staff and his cloak. He had not devoted his entire life to being godly and holy and righteous so that he could end up in a place like Nineveh! If this was supposed to be a joke, then he did not think it was very funny.…

'You will go to the great city…' continued God as Jonah marched off, '…and speak out against the evil that you will find there.'

'No!' The word was an explosion of scorn. 'What for? Everybody knows Nineveh is a wicked city! Why should I have

The dove circled above Jonah's head.

to go to a terrible place like that?'

'I want you to tell them that the Lord God knows about their wickedness.'

'No!' wailed Jonah. 'I mean, what good is it going to do? They're not going to listen to me – a foreigner. No!'

The dove tried to settle on Jonah's staff but he jerked it away. 'No. No!' he barked. 'Anyway, you're not *their* God....' He winced. What was he saying? The Lord God was supposed to be *everybody's* God. 'At least,' he hurried on, 'that's what *they* think. They've got gods of their own. Nasty heathen gods with claws and wings and horns.' He shuddered. 'I'd rather jump in the sea!' He began to walk even faster. 'No! Why should it matter to you what happens in Nineveh? It certainly doesn't matter to me!'

'Jonah....'

'It probably doesn't even matter to them!' Jonah exclaimed, waving his arms wildly. 'I'm not going! No, no, no....'

A passing stranger gawped at the madman, bolting along at top speed and shouting to himself.

Jonah hurried away from the voice of God as fast as his scrawny legs would carry him. He headed for the coast and the city of Joppa, the opposite direction to Nineveh. With any luck he would be able to find a ship that would carry him even further away.

When Jonah arrived in Joppa, he headed straight for the harbour where he found a boat being loaded with cargo, bound for the distant city of Tarshish. Mightily relieved, he scuttled down into the hold to hide in the darkness. The gentle motion of the sea soothed him like a mother rocking a child. Soon he was fast asleep.

Luckily the ship's crew did not sleep. Had they done so, they might not have been ready for the terrible storm which arose when they were far out at sea. The sky grew black, the water whirled into a frenzy, and the wind roared so violently that it snapped the mast in two. The small vessel climbed the waves as big as mountains, teetered on the crest, then crashed down into bottomless troughs. The captain and his men crawled along the pitching deck, grabbing anything that moved and throwing it overboard to lighten the load.

'There are never storms at this time of year!' the baffled

At the port of Joppa, Jonah boarded a boat to take him far away.

captain yelled.

'The ship is cursed!' shouted one of the sailors, his voice quaking with fear.

'Then pray to your gods,' the captain urged, hoping that some god somewhere might take pity on them and calm the sea.

In the hold, the cargo began to roll about like marbles on a tin tray. Jonah awoke. He heard the crashing of the waves and realized immediately that the storm was his punishment from God. He groaned. What a fool he had been to think he could hide from the Lord God! Now those poor sailors would lose their lives too. How could he have been such a simpleton?

Up on deck he found the sailors pleading with their gods for their lives, but the storm just grew worse.

'You're wasting your time,' muttered Jonah. 'It's useless.'

The captain glowered at him. 'At least you could pray to your god.'

Jonah shrugged. 'That will be useless, too.'

The sailors exchanged glances. Someone on this ship had brought them bad luck. Could it be this gloomy passenger?

The captain insisted they draw lots to find out who was to blame. He produced a handful of straws. The sailors each took one.

Jonah struggled across the deck to draw his, knowing full well that the Lord God would put the tell-tale straw into his hand.

'Who are you?' the sailors demanded angrily when they saw that Jonah had drawn the short straw. 'Where are you from?'

'I am Jonah. I am a Hebrew and I fear the Lord God.'

'Which god?'

'The Lord God of heaven who made the sea and the dry land.'

Then Jonah explained that his God was punishing him for running away, but that if he was thrown into the sea the Lord God would stop the storm.

The sailors stared at him in astonishment. Was the man crazy, asking to be thrown into the sea? A great wave hit the ship and drenched them all. No man could live for two minutes in that seething, raging water!

'Throw me overboard,' Jonah insisted.

'The gods will punish us,' objected one of the sailors, greatly alarmed.

'Do what I tell you!' roared Jonah.

Reluctantly, the captain nodded, and the sailors lowered Jonah over the side of the ship.

Jonah drew the short straw.

The moment his feet touched the water, it miraculously became calm.

The captain was relieved. 'Lift him out!'

But as they hauled Jonah up, the waves reared up with him and knocked the boat from side to side.

Again the captain ordered him to be put in the sea, and again the sea stilled itself for the brief minute that Jonah was in the water. When they dunked him a third time and found that, yet again, the sea remained calm for just as long as Jonah remained in the water, they finally understood. The storm would only stop when Jonah had been abandoned to the waves.

'Drop him...now....' ordered the captain regretfully.

Jonah was lowered into the stormy sea and suddenly it became calm.

As Jonah sank beneath the water the clouds parted, the sun came out and the sea grew smooth and blue and sparkling.

The sailors fell down on their knees to thank Jonah's God, the Lord God of heaven who had made the sea and the dry land.

Down and down Jonah spiralled through the glassy water. He could see the glimmer of the sun on the surface of the sea, high above his head. He knew the sailors were safe and he was glad for them, but even so he was frightened. His heart cried out to the Lord God as his life slipped away. So intent was he on his prayers that he hardly noticed the mammoth fish, greater than any whale, its back crusted with barnacles and rocks, swimming towards him like an island of dry land. He scarcely realized what was happening when he was wafted in through the fish's mouth, swept along by a tangle of dark ribbon seaweed right into the creature's belly. All he knew was that the sun no longer shone through the surface of the sea.

'Hear me, Jonah, and listen to what I say,' said the voice of God as Jonah lay helpless inside the fish.

Seaweed bound Jonah's feet like a gravecloth as he prayed.

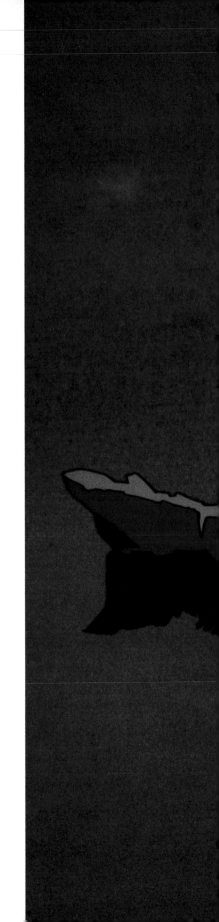

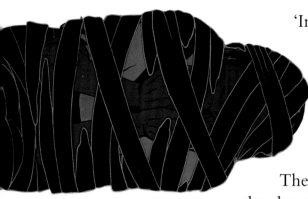

Inside the great fish, seaweed wrapped itself around Jonah's body.

'In my distress I called to the Lord!'

'And He heard your voice,' God reassured him.

'When the waves closed over me and my life seemed to be at an end, I cried out....'

'And He answered you.'

The weed continued to wrap around him, like a shawl swaddling a baby.

'As I sank to the ocean depths,' Jonah sighed, 'I remembered the Lord....'

'And He saved your life,' God replied.

Jonah frowned. Saved his life? Had the Lord God really saved his life? How strange...because, actually, he did not seem to be alive anymore. The seaweed had covered his face like a shroud. He could no longer move, could no longer see....

As Jonah lay motionless, the great fish moved swiftly through the sea. And then, in the shallows, the fish spewed out the man on to the shore.

Jonah tore the seaweed from his face and looked out to sea at the great fish basking nearby, flapping its tail in the sun. He was alive after all.

Then he peered down at himself. Oh, would you believe it! His sandals had been lost in the water, his shirt too. Irritably, he looked around for a stick.

'Yes, you are still in one piece,' God reminded him dryly. 'So pick up your staff and start walking!'

This time Jonah did as he was told. He walked and walked, all the long way to Nineveh. As soon as he stepped through the gates he could see that the rumours had been right. The place was seething with wickedness. Boys battled, thieves thieved and pick-pockets picked pockets, right out on the streets for anyone to see.

'People of Nineveh…' rebuked the wide-eyed Jonah, 'I bring a terrible message for your city. The Lord God whom I serve….'

A pair of beggars jeered at him. A mother, surrounded by her children, stared insolently. Had he not seen the immense statue of Ishtar? It had to be the biggest statue in the world. 'We've got our own gods,' she sneered. 'And the greatest of them all is mighty Ishtar.'

Jonah saw that Nineveh was corrupt and that the people worshipped their own gods.

Jonah was dragged
to the King's palace
by two soldiers.

'The Lord my God says…' Jonah struggled to make himself heard above the din.

Two soldiers watched him ranting, their arms folded.

'The Lord my God says…!' shouted Jonah.

One of the soldiers winked at the other.

'The Lord my God has told me…'

The soldiers began to pace menacingly towards Jonah.

'to tell you…'

With a hefty blow they knocked him to the ground.

'…that he has seen your sins,' persisted Jonah as they grabbed his arms and dragged him through the streets. 'And in forty days he will destroy Nineveh!'

Those bystanders who heard him howled with laughter. 'Destroy great Nineveh? He'll have a job.'

At the sound of laughter Jonah's temper snapped. How dare they jeer at the Lord God! The Lord God had saved his life! Indeed at this very moment the Lord God was trying to save their lives – and all they could do was laugh! Well, he had not spent his entire life trying to be good only to be mocked by a bunch of criminals. 'The Lord God knows all your sins!' he roared.

The people tried to shrug off his words, but they could see fire in Jonah's eyes and it made them uneasy. They looked at one another. Could there really be a god who knew all about their sins? No…. It was not possible….

As the soldiers pulled him towards the palace, Jonah stared at all the sinners he passed. He saw people stealing from each other as they crossed paths, men throttling each other in dark corners, children defying their mothers, mothers beating their children. He saw them all. And they saw him. They saw the fire in his eyes and their stomachs lurched.

'The Lord God has seen the sins on the streets on Nineveh!' Jonah shouted at them. 'He has seen the corruption in your temple…and in the palace of your great King.'

The people grew worried. He couldn't be right, could he? No! No! Of course not. The gods of Nineveh were carved from stone. They had stone eyes and stone hearts. They could not see. They did not care.

The King of Nineveh.

At last Jonah arrived at the palace of the King of Nineveh. He was forced to kneel before the throne.

The King looked at his courtiers. 'Why does he threaten my people with punishments from a god whom we know nothing about?' he drawled.

'Because the Lord God knows each and every one of you,' Jonah snapped back. 'And the wicked lives you lead.'

'What does your god know?' the King asked uneasily.

'Everything.'

'What is to happen to us?'

'Because of Nineveh's sinfulness, the Lord God is going to destroy this entire city in forty days!'

And then the King himself saw the fire in Jonah's eyes.

In that fire he saw the flames that would consume his great city, the flames that would send the temples and palaces tumbling down. In Jonah's eyes he saw the wrath of God, and when he saw it he understood that there was a God who saw, a God who cared.

The King turned away and went behind a curtain. When he emerged, his regal robes had been replaced by coarse hessian. Ashes streaked his face. 'In Nineveh,' he said, 'when someone dies, those who are in mourning put on sackcloth and smear their faces with ashes. If, in forty days, we are all dead, then it will be too late to mourn.'

Then he sent out a proclamation to all Nineveh: 'No person or animal,' it decreed, 'herd or flock, may eat anything. Everyone, man and beast, must be covered in sackcloth and the people must call on the Lord God who made heaven and earth with all their might, asking for forgiveness.'

The people of Nineveh did as they were told. They prayed to the God of the man with fire in his eyes. And as they prayed they felt, for the first time in their lives, that someone heard, someone saw, someone cared.

Jonah was triumphant. He, Jonah, had told these wicked people what was what! He was the one who had notified them of God's intentions! He gloated to see the streets filled with

people dressed in sackcloth, on their knees, pleading with the Lord God for their very lives. Proudly, Jonah set off for a hill overlooking the city where he would have a fine view of the destruction when it came!

At the top of the hill he made a pile of stones, like a little Nineveh, and imagined it crumbling to dust. 'When God's

The people of Nineveh covered themselves in sackcloth and ate no food.

Jonah went to the top of a hill and waited for God's anger to destroy Nineveh.

anger falls,' he muttered righteously, glaring at the stones, 'it will be as if it had never existed!'

On the fortieth day, God's anger appeared in the sky. Great clouds gathered, ominous winds stirred the air, great forks of lightning crackled overhead.

Jonah strutted back and forth on his hilltop. 'Lord God!' he cried. 'Bring down your judgment! Now!'

In the streets of the city the people poured out their prayers. 'God in heaven do not destroy us! Pity and save us! Lord God forgive us! Have mercy on us! Do not destroy us! Pity and save us!'

God heard them and He was moved. He sent a shaft of sunlight through the black clouds to shine on the people of Nineveh. The wind tore at their sackcloth coverings and blew them away.

'We have been saved!' they cried. 'God be praised!' 'We are alive!'

Jonah glowered at the sun-bathed city in disbelief. He had never felt such a fool in all his life! 'I should have known this would happen,' he growled through clenched teeth. 'This is the fortieth day...the day on which I prophesied the Lord God's judgment would come, and what happens? Nothing!'

He glared up at the sky. 'You wondered why I didn't obey you when you first told me to go to Nineveh! Well,' he howled, 'this is why!'

Jonah shook his head in frustration. 'I knew that you were a tender, compassionate and merciful God, slow to be angry and full of love; the kind of God who would change His mind and forgive the people of Nineveh!'

God did not reply.

'So why don't you take my life?' Jonah implored. 'I was your prophet and I've been made to look a fool! It would be better for me if I were dead!'

'Are you right to be this angry?' God said quizzically.

'Yes!' Jonah screeched. 'Yes I am!' I shall sit here and wait

When the people of Nineveh repented their sins, God saved them from destruction.

Jonah ate berries from the tree which God had sent to shelter him.

until either judgment falls on Nineveh, or until I die of shame!'

Jonah lay down on the bare ground and waited to die. Infuriatingly, he was still alive when night fell.

Even more annoyingly, he slept all night. And to crown it all, when he woke up, God, who knew how much Jonah loved to sit in the shade of a tree, had made a tree grow up to shelter him! Oh, this was too much....

Grudgingly, Jonah ate berries from the tree, drank dew from its leaves, sat in its shade and waited for either death or destruction to arrive – preferably death!

However, he did not imagine that it would be the tree that would die. When he awoke on the second morning, he found that caterpillars had feasted on his tree in the night and killed it.

'Oh no!' he wailed. 'Why are you treating me this way?'

Clouds of butterflies rose up from the tree and made a golden canopy over his head. He scowled at them. Wretched butterflies! 'First you give me a plant to shade me from the heat,' he reproached, 'then you destroy it! Why? I might as well be dead!'

He fell to his knees. 'Let me die, now,' he begged. 'Just as you let that plant die.'

'Are you really right to be so angry about the plant?' God asked wryly.

'Yes! I have every right to be angry. Angry enough to die!'

'You feel sorry for a mere plant that you did not grow, a plant that grew up and withered away in just one day, a plant which cost you nothing….'

Rain pattered down on the dry earth like tear-drops, as if to remind Jonah that nothing grew without God's help. He frowned.

A cloud of butterflies rose up over Jonah's head.

'So Jonah,' asked God, 'shouldn't I feel sorry for a whole city of people – more than one hundred and twenty thousand of my creations – who do not know right from wrong?'

Jonah hung his head. The rain fell in a torrent,

surrounding him with water. It reminded Jonah of the sea from which God had so kindly saved him. He looked at Nineveh. A beautiful rainbow shone above the city. Even *he* had to admit that Nineveh looked worth saving now.

As Jonah cringed with shame, children came out of the city and climbed the hill. They encircled him, smiling lovingly at the man who had saved them from death. They did not seem to think he was a fool.

To his surprise Jonah found himself smiling back. Well, well.... Children would not have dared behave like that when he was a lad. How odd. Perhaps the world was becoming a better place after all....

RUTH

Naomi was crying. The tears ran down her face and into her mouth. They tasted of salt and sadness.

Her two grown-up sons were dead. They had been brought to their father's grave, a small cave in a rocky hillside, and laid tenderly beside him on the ground. Now Naomi knelt in the cave, saying her last goodbye. A small lamp glowed softly, allowing her to see her sons for the last time.

Even though they were wrapped in white linen, she could recognize them. Their features were as familiar to her as the palms of her own hands.

She remembered seeing them for the first time when they had just been born. They had blinked at the light. They had waved their little hands in the air, reaching out for their mother as all new babies do. She had loved them so much, and had gone on loving them just as much as they grew into men. She could not bear to think of them dead, lying forever beside their father in this grave.

Naomi would have crumpled to the floor had it not been for the two brave young women whose arms came around her to support her.

'I'm sorry,' she sobbed. 'I should be comforting you, not the other way round. You're young. You've both lost your husbands.... You loved them so.... And now you're left with nothing.'

Ruth and Orpah comforted their mother-in-law, Naomi.

One of them, Ruth, stroked Naomi's brow. 'But you've had so many troubles to face,' she said. 'It's not long since your own husband, Elimelech, died…. Just when you thought everything was getting better at last.'

Naomi nodded sadly. 'Elimelech was so pleased that we had settled down well here in Moab. He hated taking us from Bethlehem to a foreign country, but what choice did he have? It didn't rain. All the crops stopped growing, the soil on our land turned to dust. We were starving – everyone in Bethlehem was starving. Everyone in the whole of Judea! We had to find somewhere where there was food.' She put her hands to her face and pressed her eyes to stop the tears. 'Maybe it would have been better if we'd stayed in our own country and starved.'

'Don't say that,' whispered Ruth. 'You brought our husbands to Moab. We wouldn't have met them if you hadn't come here.'

Orpah took Naomi's hand. 'We loved your sons just as we love you.'

Naomi smiled. 'May the Lord God bless you. My sons couldn't have chosen better wives.'

When a great stone had been rolled across the mouth of the cave, closing the grave for ever, Naomi gazed out over the plains of Moab. Then she turned her eyes up to the vast evening sky and the red melting sun. She imagined the people of Judea, her own people, gazing up at that same sun. All that divided the two countries was the Great Salt Sea. She had walked around that sea to get here, and she would walk around it again to get back home.

'I must return to Bethlehem,' she said.

The young women were shocked. 'But why, Naomi?'

'God's hand is against me,' she sighed. 'Our family name has ended here in Moab.'

Naomi and Ruth left Moab together.

Ruth and Orpah understood her pain. Naomi's people believed that family names were important. If Naomi had only had a grandson then the name would have lived on.

'We're coming with you,' said Ruth.

Naomi shook her head but Orpah protested. 'It's far too dangeous for a woman to go alone!'

'But what more can I suffer?' Naomi cried. 'I've already lost everything!'

'You still have us,' Ruth reminded her.

Naomi blinked back fresh tears. How she would love to keep them with her – but she had to put their well-being first. 'You must stay here with your own people,' she insisted. 'You're still young, you can marry again.'

The young women knew that if they went with Naomi they would never find new husbands. Moab and Judea were often at war, and anyway, the Judeans expected a widow to marry the nearest male in the family, usually the brother of her dead husband.

'I have no more sons to offer you,' Naomi said sadly.

Orpah bit her lip. Life would be very empty without a child. Men tended their fields and women tended their children.... That was how life had been since the beginning of time. She could not imagine living forever without a husband, without a child. Hard as it was to leave her dear mother-in-law, Orpah felt there was no choice. She would stay in Moab and find a new husband. 'We'll never forget you,' she promised Naomi. 'Never.' Tears stung her eyes as she turned her back and walked away.

But Ruth could not bring herself to go. What if Naomi came to harm on the journey back? What if there was still famine in Judea? Ruth could not let her mother-in-law face the future alone.

'Follow your sister, Ruth,' Naomi urged. 'Go back to your mother.'

'No!' Ruth's eyes burned with love. 'You are my mother now! Where you go, I will go, and where you live, I will live. Your people will be my people and your God my God. Where you die, I will die, and there I will be buried.'

Naomi was stunned by the loyalty in Ruth's words – and the love in her eyes. She did not argue further.

Day after day, the two women trudged across the wilderness towards Bethlehem. To their relief the famine was over, the drought had ended. Judea was lush and green again and the people were well fed. And when the two women stepped through the gates of Bethlehem, women clustered around Naomi, shouting greetings, asking questions.

'Where's your husband? Your sons?'

'Can the earth give up its dead?' Naomi replied heavily.

The women were appalled. 'God have mercy,' one gasped. 'All dead?'

Naomi and Ruth
entered the gates
of Bethlehem
and the women
of the town
clustered around
them.

'Speak of sorrow, not mercy,' Naomi muttered. 'Because God has dealt so bitterly with me.' She took Ruth's hand. 'She is all I have now. Ruth. Wife of my eldest son.'

The women stared uneasily at Ruth. She looked different from them, darker-skinned, as Moabites were. They thought her very strange. Ruth felt embarrassed. She did not know what to say.

But then a little boy came dancing up to them, waving a stick. He hurtled into Ruth who put out a hand to steady him. He looked up at her and smiled sweetly. Ruth bent down and stroked his head. Children were the same the world over – they did not care about people's differences, only their kindnesses. A lump rose in Ruth's throat. She had dreamed of having a little boy of her own one day, a little boy just like this one…. But it would not happen now, would it?

Naomi grieved to see the stricken look in Ruth's eyes. She understood how much Ruth had given up by coming with her.

When Naomi and Ruth reached Naomi's old house, they

saw that it had become dirty and broken-down after being empty for so long. Naomi's friends and neighbours were shocked that the two women planned to live there, but Ruth took her mother-in-law's arm. 'This is my home too,' she said with dignity. 'I live wherever Naomi lives now.'

They had a roof over their heads but the rooms were cold and bare and they had nothing except the clothes they stood up in. The food they had brought with them from Moab was almost gone. The nearby fields, however, were golden with barley. The spring harvest had already begun.

At dawn on their first morning in Bethlehem, Naomi gave her last crust of bread to Ruth. She felt ashamed that she had nothing else to offer the girl who had given up so much to stay with her.

'I'm going to the fields to glean,' Ruth announced.

Naomi was shocked. Only very poor people gleaned, crawling behind the harvesters, scrabbling in the dirt for any stray ears of corn which fell to the ground. 'Scavenging with the poor,' she protested. 'Oh, my child....'

'We are poor,' Ruth said wryly.

Naomi gave
Ruth her last
crust of bread.

'But the men who are harvesting...' Naomi pulled a face. Oh dear. The men would not treat Ruth with respect once they saw she was a foreigner. 'They could take advantage of you,' she warned.

Ruth knew Naomi was right, but she would not show that she was afraid. 'I'll be careful,' she assured Naomi.

'You're such a stubborn child,' Naomi scolded lovingly. 'A child should listen to her mother!'

'A daughter should work so her mother can eat,' Ruth teased in return.

'Perhaps....' Naomi gave Ruth a hug. 'May the Lord God keep you safe.'

Naomi was right about the men. They jeered at Ruth because she was a Moabite. They accused her of being a thief and a

Each day, the men from Bethlehem gathered in the fields to harvest the corn.

beggar – and worse. Even the steward snorted in disgust when she begged to be allowed to glean.

'Please,' she implored, desperate to find a little barley to take back to the empty house. 'If not for my sake, for my mother-in-law, Naomi.'

The foreman overheard them from his seat high on a camel's back. He frowned at Ruth. 'So you're the Moabite woman who came back with Naomi?'

'Yes.' Ruth's heart was pounding but she looked bravely up at the man.

'Well, what are you doing here?' He pointed into the distance. 'Her land lies over there.'

Ruth tried not to get angry. Surely he knew that Naomi had not been here to plant any seed? 'That land lies barren,' she explained. 'Please let me glean here.'

'I can't give you permission. This land belongs to Boaz.'

'Then let me glean till he arrives! Believe me, I'll not keep a single grain without his consent.'

The foreman thought for a moment. 'Oh, all right. But keep well back from the others. They won't want you joining them.'

'The Lord God bless you,' said Ruth. Suddenly she felt very glad that she had taken the God of the Jews for her own. She felt sure He would protect her. As a child in Moab she had been taught to worship many gods, but she had never felt that they cared for her at all.

As the sun rose high in the sky, Boaz came to see how the work was progressing. His eye was caught by a lone figure still gleaning, although everyone else had retired to the shade for their midday meal. He shaded his eyes to see the young woman better. As she stooped to pick up a single grain, his heart ached with pity.

The foreman came forward to explain his agreement with

Ruth. 'She's a hard worker,' he added. 'She hasn't stopped all morning.'

Boaz poured a drink of water from one of his pitchers and took the cup out into the field to Ruth.

'Here,' he said, offering it to her. 'You must be thirsty.'

Ruth turned bewildered eyes on Boaz. 'My lord, why do you show me such kindness?'

'Because I have heard all that you have done for Naomi. You deserve a rich reward.' He handed her the cup which she took gratefully. The sun was hot and she had not dared stop work to go to the well.

'All I can do', he continued, 'is give you permission to glean wherever you like.'

Ruth lowered her eyes. 'You are most generous.'

Boaz looked thoughtfully at the modest young woman. 'Ruth,' he said at last. 'Work only on my land so that I can make sure that no man troubles you.'

Then he led her off to eat with his dumbfounded workers. When they gave her bread, Boaz noticed that she saved some for Naomi.

Before he left, he took one of his men aside. 'Take some ears from the pile of grain,' he said softly, 'and drop them in her path.'

It was well after dark when Ruth arrived home.

Naomi had been dreadfully worried, but she was delighted when she saw how much grain Ruth had brought.

'And there's more!' Ruth laughed, producing the bread. 'He let me share their meal and I saved some for you.'

'He let…who let you?' Naomi demanded.

Ruth lit the fire before she answered. 'His name is Boaz,' she revealed with a smile. 'And he said I could glean for the whole harvest.'

Naomi put her hand to her throat. 'The Lord God guided you to Boaz, I am certain of it. He owns many fields. And he's a close kinsman of ours. A cousin of my dead husband! May the Lord God bless him for his kindness.'

As Naomi put away the barley she thought about Boaz. Although she knew he was both wise and fair, she had never known him show such kindness to a stranger before....

Every day, Ruth toiled under the hot sun until all the barley had been safely gathered in, and then all through the wheat harvest, too. As the weeks passed, Boaz noticed how hard Ruth worked for her mother-in-law. He admired her very much.

Naomi was full of admiration for Ruth, too. How would she have managed if Ruth had stayed behind? Oh, if only she could do something for Ruth in return. Something that would make Ruth happy for the rest of her life....

By the end of the harvest, Ruth had brought home a vast amount of grain. Naomi was puzzled. How could anyone gather so much just from gleaning? Boaz was good to his men, but surely he would not let them be so careless as to drop this much? Perhaps he had wanted to ensure that the two women did not go hungry, but in that case why did he not simply give them some food? It did not make sense. Unless, perhaps, he had a special reason for wanting Ruth to work near him all day.

When Ruth came home after her last day in the fields she chattered happily about finding fresh work now that the harvest was over.

'You won't find many employers as generous as Boaz,' Naomi remarked.

'No, I'll miss...', then to Naomi's surprise, Ruth cut the sentence short 'I'll miss working on his land,' she mumbled at last. But she would not meet Naomi's eye when she said it, and

although the light was not very good in the house, Naomi was certain that Ruth was blushing.

Naomi's mind raced. Now she came to think of it, Ruth often looked away when she spoke of Boaz.

The door rattled on its hinges.

'There's a good breeze tonight,' Naomi said thoughtfully – the wind helped the winnowers by blowing the dust and chaff from the grain. 'Boaz will be winnowing long after nightfall again…. So he'll eat and sleep outdoors.' She met her daughter-in-law's eye. 'Ruth, you must speak with him tonight, alone.'

Naomi urged Ruth to speak to Boaz that night.

163

'Why?'

'He's a relation of ours,' Naomi explained. Indeed, Boaz was close enough in law to be considered next-of-kin, close enough to take a brother's place. 'Ruth, if you would only ask him, I know he would honour his duty by marrying you.'

'Marry me?' Ruth could hardly get the words out, her mouth was so dry. 'But I'm a foreigner and a widow.'

Naomi saw pride flash across Ruth's face and knew that Ruth would never ask Boaz. She was convinced he would not want her.

Naomi prayed the Lord God's forgiveness for her next words. 'If you were to have a child together...' she said, knowing full well that Ruth would do anything for her mother-in-law, 'our family name would be restored.'

Ruth could hardly breathe. What was Naomi saying? That it was her duty to ask Boaz to marry her for Naomi's sake, so that the family name would not die out? Her hands began to tremble. 'Tell me what I must do,' she breathed.

'First,' said Naomi briskly, 'we must prepare you.' She brought water for Ruth to wash, and began to anoint Ruth's hair with perfumed oil.

'No one must see you together,' she said. 'Wait until everyone is asleep, then go and lie near him. Uncover his feet. He'll wake later with the cold and...well, he will tell you what to do.'

Ruth was shivering with a mixture of fear and excitement as she hurried through the night to the fields. She knew Boaz would turn her down – she was only going for Naomi's sake – *but what if he said yes?*

Hidden by the darkness, she watched Boaz sitting silently by the fire while his men celebrated the harvest with music and

laughter. At last everyone lay down to sleep. Boaz lay alone beside one of the mounds of grain. Ruth waited until she was certain that everybody was asleep, then she tiptoed out from her hiding-place. She was quaking with fear as she drew back the covering from his feet.

She lay on the hard earth, frightened that he would not wake. But Naomi, as ever, was right. In the chill of the night Boaz did stir, and as he awakened he became aware that someone was at his feet.

'Who are you?' he asked, peering into the darkness.

'Ruth, my lord.' Panic gripped her, and it took a few moments for her to collect herself. She could hardly bring herself to speak the next words, but at last she found the courage. 'Spread the corner of your garment over me,' she whispered, 'for you are my next of kin.'

Boaz sat frozen in the darkness. Could this really be happening? Could Ruth, the young woman who had impressed the whole of Bethlehem with her loyalty and her courage, could she really be asking *him* to do this for her? And then with a jolt of dismay he realized that she had only asked him for Naomi's sake – not because she loved him. 'May God reward you,' he said. 'Such a sacrifice for Naomi's sake is great indeed.' He swallowed. 'You have earned the respect of many. You could have married for love.'

Ruth almost blurted out that she did indeed love him, but she was afraid he would laugh at her.

'Anyway, I am not free to marry you,' Boaz continued gently. 'There is another kinsman, closer in line.' According to the laws of Judea this man had the right to marry Ruth if he chose. 'He must give his consent before I can do what you ask…. But we must wait until morning.'

When dawn broke, he woke her and urged her to go before

Naomi reassured
Ruth that Boaz
would marry her.

anyone saw them together. He gave her barley for Naomi. 'Reassure her that the matter will be settled with honour,' he said. 'Whatever the outcome, you will have a husband today.'

Ruth's eyes smarted as she stumbled back to Bethlehem. How she wished she had never gone! By the end of the day she could be married to some man whom she had never even met!

'Why didn't you tell me we had another kinsman closer in line!' she reproached as Naomi came forward to greet her.

'There is no kinsman more worthy than Boaz!' Naomi insisted.

'He is certainly a man of great honour,' said Ruth.

Naomi patted her comfortingly on the shoulder. 'Boaz is as wise as he is good,' she consoled. 'He will not let another man make you his bride.'

Ruth sighed. How could Boaz marry her if the law said she should marry another man? She did not understand.

But Naomi understood. She knew that while laws must not be broken, sometimes they can be bent.

Boaz was trying to think of a way to bend the law, but he could not. He knew that the moment he told his kinsman that he wanted Ruth for himself, then he would lose her. The man was greedy. If he thought something was valuable he snatched it.

As Boaz walked to the city gates of Bethlehem he racked his brains. He had to settle this matter honourably, but how could he be honourable and still ensure that he became Ruth's husband?

As soon as his kinsman came by, he called him over. 'We have something to discuss,' he said.

Boaz studied the crowd of curious people which began to gather around him, and was pleased to see that there were a number of elders present who would be able to bear witness to his proposal. But then his gaze fell on Ruth and Naomi, standing together a little way off, and his heart began to thud. What if he failed? What if the elders ended up bearing witness to the marriage of Ruth and his greedy kinsman? He could hardly bear to think of it.

He took a deep breath and turned to his kinsman. 'You are of Elimelech's clan, like me,' he said firmly. 'Now, his widow, Naomi, has put her land up for sale. If you wish to buy the land, and honour the obligations which accompany it, tell us now. If

Boaz told his kinsman that Naomi's land was up for sale.

you do not, I myself will buy it since I am next in line after you.'

The kinsman's eyes lit up when Boaz mentioned that he would like the land. 'I will buy it,' the man said quickly.

'You do realize', continued Boaz carefully, 'that on the day you buy the land you also buy Ruth, the widow of Elimelech's elder son? You must do this in order to revive the family name.' He deliberately did not say that he wanted Ruth himself.

The kinsman frowned. Land…. Yes, he wanted the land that Boaz was so keen on…. But some widow for a wife? That was another matter.

'You'll have children,' warned a bystander. 'And they'll have first claim on the land, not you.'

'And on your other property, no doubt,' muttered someone else.

The kinsman was alarmed. 'Then I cannot. Boaz, take my right yourself,' he insisted. Quickly, he dragged off his shoe and thrust it into Boaz' hand – an old tradition which indicated that a deal had been struck. 'Before the elders here, I recognize your right to walk upon our kinswoman's land,' he proclaimed.

Boaz gripped the shoe so hard that his knuckles blanched. He waved it above his head. 'You are witnesses that I now buy from Naomi everything which belonged to Elimelech. Also I…' He hesitated. He was not *buying* Ruth…he did not want anyone to think that his future wife

Boaz held up the shoe and the agreement was sealed.

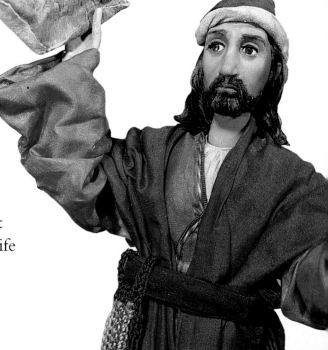

could be bought and sold! 'Also,' he continued,' Ruth the Moabitess, I take as my wife!'

From out of the crowd came a cry. Boaz saw Ruth looking at him with wide eyes. Had she cried out in dismay? Did she not want him? His heart sank.

Boaz did not see Ruth again until the sun was setting and she was brought to his house dressed in her wedding finery. As she walked towards him she kept her eyes cast down. It tore at his heart that she would not look at him, but at last she did look up. She looked right into his eyes — and he saw her love for him burning there as unmistakeably as it had burned on the day she had taken Naomi's people for her own. And when Boaz offered her his hand, she took it so eagerly that any last doubts melted away.

When the spring harvest came again, Ruth became a mother. She laid the newborn baby in Naomi's arms.

'You have a son once more,' she said gently.

The baby blinked at the light; his little hands waved in the air as he reached for his grandmother. Naomi's

Naomi took Ruth's child, Obed, in her arms.

eyes filled with tears of happiness.

All the neighbours came in. These days they loved Ruth almost as much as Naomi did. They crowded round the baby.

'May the Lord God bless him,' they said. One of them begged her to call him Obed.

Naomi smiled down at Ruth's child. 'Obed!' she said. 'The servant of the Lord.'

And indeed Obed did serve the Lord, because when he grew up he became the father of Jesse, and Jesse became the father of David, and David became King of all Israel.

E L I J A H

W hen the soldiers marched through the streets of Samaria the entire city trembled.

The soldiers took silver, rings, cooking-pots – anything they could lay their hands on.

When the houses had been stripped bare, when everything had been taken, the people told themselves that at least they were safe, that the soldiers would not come again.

But the soldiers did come again. And when they found there was nothing left, they took lives.

The prophet Elijah.

Elijah could smell fear every time he passed through the city gates. Since Ahab had come to the throne, all Israel reeked of it – but the stench was strongest in Samaria, the city King Ahab's father had created from a bare hill. Ahab continued to build, determined that one day his city would be greater even than Jerusalem, determined that the money would be found to make it happen.

The King's new buildings cast long shadows, and in those shadows crept the poor people who had paid for it all. Could Ahab smell the fear, Elijah wondered, up there in his great palace? Could he hear the screams as

King Ahab and
Jezebel of Sidon
were married
before the high
priest of Baal.

his soldiers kicked and beat and slashed and killed?

Elijah did not fear King Ahab. But then Elijah was not like
most men. While others cowered behind locked doors, the
prophet Elijah roamed the wild places, the rocks and ravines of
the wilderness, far from the city, so that he would be ready to
hear the voice of the Lord God when it came.

Koning Achab aanbad een god zonder stem, een god die Baäl heette. Hij aanbad Baäl omdat hij met Izebel wilde trouwen, de dochter van de hogepriester van Baäl. Om haar te verleiden had hij een tempel laten bouwen, een heilige struik laten planten en in de tempel beelden van Baäl laten neerzetten, enorme standbeelden met angstaanjagende hoorns. Tijdens de huwelijksplechtigheid van koning Achab en Izebel van Sidon werd het volk van Israël gedwongen voor de god Baäl te knielen. Ze deden wat hun was opgedragen omdat ze bang waren.

De profeten van de Here God waren echter niet bang. Toen Achab knielde om de voeten van de afgod te kussen, kwamen twee van hen naar voren en riepen: 'In de naam van de Here, de God van Israël...'

'Grijp hen!' beval Izebel.

Toen de priester van Baäl de twee haveloze mannen had laten grijpen, hoonde Izebel: 'Wie is deze Here, de God van Israël?'

'Eh... het koninkrijk Israël is groot,' stotterde Achab. 'Er is toch genoeg plaats voor alle goden?'

Izebel keek haar nieuwe man minachtend aan. Toen beval ze dat iedere profeet van de Here God gedood moest worden.

Ze werden met honderden tegelijk afgeslacht. Elia, die door het ruige landschap ten oosten van de Jordaan trok, vond overal met bloed doordrenkte lichamen op de kale rotsen en knielde overmand door verdriet naast hen neer.

Maar terwijl hij daar neerknielde begon zijn huid te prikkelen. Het woord van God kwam tot hem, omcirkelde hem. De stem van God was nog niet hoorbaar, maar het woord was helder en duidelijk. Het was overal; in de lucht die hij inademde, in de aarde onder zijn voeten, in de hemel boven hem.

'Ga naar Achab, want de Here zegt dat er een grote droogte komt.'

Elia haastte zich naar het paleis. Hij negeerde de bewakers en liep in zijn kameelharen mantel met gezwinde spoed door de gangen,

swiftly through the corridors. Cloaked in his coarse mantle of camel-hair, Elijah threw back rich damask curtains and entered the throne room. The entire court froze at the sight of the wild man standing before them.

'As the Lord the God of Israel lives,' he said, his voice more rich and compelling than any voice they had ever heard, 'there shall not be dew nor rain these years...'

Queen Jezebel sprang to her feet, her face scored with hatred. But anything she might have said was drowned by the powerful resonance of Elijah's words, as he roared: '...but according to His word!'

Then he turned on his heel and strode out.

Jezebel stared at the yawning space he had left. 'Who is this?' she hissed. 'Who defies my Lord Baal, the rain-maker?'

'It is Elijah,' Ahab explained nervously. 'A prophet of the Lord God of Israel.'

Jezebel's eyes narrowed. 'Then find the blasphemer and bring him to me!'

But for once the soldiers could not obey their queen. No matter how much they searched they could not find the last prophet of Israel.

And in all the weeks that they searched for Elijah not a drop of rain fell, not a whisper of dew came to moisten the earth. The plants withered, the ground cracked wide.

Elijah roamed the wilderness, parched, ravenous, listening endlessly for the faint echo of soldiers' voices. Then the word of God came again, came from the scorching rocks and the spiralling dust, and fell like powder on his skin.

'Hide yourself by the brook of Cherith. The Lord will feed you there.'

When Elijah reached the brook he found to his astonishment

Izebel was razend van woede. Dag na dag liet ze de soldaten door het barre landschap trekken en uiteindelijk vonden ze een stukje van Elia's mantel dat aan een doorn was blijven hangen. De soldaten begonnen het spoor naar de Kerit te volgen.

Plotseling droogde de beek op. De raven waren niet meer dan een stipje in de lucht.

Elia stond doodstil. Deze keer kwam het woord via de kreten van de vogels, via de zware voetstappen van de soldaten in de verte en het zachte trillen van de rivierbedding.

'Ga naar Sarfat in het land Sidon...'

Sidon? Elia kon zijn oren niet geloven. Sidon was de geboorteplaats van Izebel. Sidon was het koninkrijk van Baäl.

'Ga weg uit Israël. De Here heeft een weduwe daar opdracht gegeven je te eten te geven.'

En dus verliet Elia zijn land en trok naar Sidon. Sarfat was een arme stad, verdord door de droogte en in de straten lagen de uitgemergelde lichamen van de stervenden. Maar er was wel eten in de stad. Goed eten. Het lag hoog opgestapeld op gouden schalen en was neergezet voor de standbeelden, waar het wegrotte. En terwijl de kinderen huilden van de dorst, besprenkelden de priesters van Baäl de stenen beelden van hun god met fris water.

Elia keek hoe een uitgeputte jonge vrouw takken verzamelde. Een kleine jongen strompelde zwakjes achter haar aan.

'Haal wat water voor me zodat ik kan drinken,' zei Elia die voor haar ging staan.

De weduwe schrok op door de heilige man. 'Water?' herhaalde ze zwakjes.

'En breng me een stukje brood.'

De vrouw schudde haar hoofd. Ze keek zenuwachtig naar een beeld van Baäl en fluisterde toen: 'Bij de Here God die u in uw land dient, zeg ik u dat ik niets meer heb dan een handvol meel in een

In Zarephath, as God had said, Elijah met a widow.

'And bring me a scrap of bread.'

The woman shook her head. She glanced nervously at a statue of Baal, then whispered, 'By the Lord God whom you serve in your land, I swear I have nothing but a handful of meal in a jar and a drop of oil in a jug.' She gestured at the boy, then added, 'We will eat one last meal and die.'

Elijah put his hand on her shoulder. 'Fear not,' he said. 'Go and prepare the meal, but first bake something for me. For the Lord God of Israel says: your jar of meal shall not be emptied, your jar of oil shall not fail, until the day that the Lord God sends rain upon the earth.'

The despairing woman nodded. What could it hurt, anyway, if she gave her last food to this man? She and her son would simply die a few hours sooner.

At home she mixed her last few drops of oil with the paltry handful of meal and set the cake to bake. But as she turned away from the fire her stomach lurched. Something had just happened, she was sure. She hurried to inspect her jars. They were full to overflowing.

Elijah lodged in the upper room of the widow's house for three years. In all that time the jars never emptied.

The child grew strong and healthy. But one day he clutched his head and cried out in pain. As the widow ran to tend him he collapsed in her arms and died.

Elijah heard her howl of anguish and came running.

'What have I done to you, O man of God,' she wept. 'What have I done?'

Elijah fell to his knees beside her.

'The gods have taken their revenge,' she sobbed.

'No!' roared Elijah, taking the limp body of the child in his arms and hurrying upstairs to his room.

He placed the boy on his bed and laid his hands on the child's ribs. 'O Lord God,' he reproached. 'Have you brought calamity even upon this poor widow?' He put his hands on the child again. 'Will you, Lord, let her child die?' he asked in disbelief.

'No, no....' He touched the boy for the third time. And then the rib-cage moved beneath his palms as the child drew in a

'Nu weet ik dat u een man van God bent en dat het Woord van de Here in uw mond de waarheid is!' zei ze met tranen in haar ogen.

Toen op een dag kwam het Woord tot Elia in Sarfat, uit het licht van de brandende zon en de dorre aarde onder zijn voeten. *'Ga naar Achab en ik zal het weer laten regenen...'*

En zo begon Elia de lange wandeling terug naar Israël.

Achab was met zijn soldaten op zoek naar water toen Elia voor hem verscheen.

Het hart van de koning begon te bonzen. 'Ben jij dat?' vroeg hij hees. 'Jij, die in Israël problemen brengt?'

'Ik heb Israël geen problemen gebracht,' antwoordde Elia boos. 'Jij bent de schuldige, omdat je de geboden van de Here in de wind hebt geslagen en de afgod Baäl vereert.'

Achab wendde zijn hoofd af. 'Al drie jaar lang heeft het niet geregend,' mompelde hij. 'Ik heb naar alle koninkrijken in het oosten boodschappers gestuurd om naar je te zoeken.'

Elia keek Achab spottend aan. Als Achab dacht dat Baäl een einde aan de droogte kon maken, waarom liet hij dan overal naar hem, een profeet van God, zoeken?

'Nu,' beval Elia, 'stuur je boodschappers door je eigen koninkrijk en breng alle Israëlieten bij mij op de berg Karmel – en ook alle profeten van Baäl.'

De wegen stroomden vol toen duizenden uitgehongerde mensen naar de Karmel kwamen en moeizaam de rotsachtige berg beklommen.

'Is dat de koning?' vroeg een oude man die naar Achab wees.

'Ik geloof het wel,' antwoordde een jongeman die zijn vader het steile pad op hielp. 'Laten we bidden dat Elia vandaag een einde aan zijn slechtheid maakt. Izebel en Achab hebben heel Israël bang gemaakt met hun verafgoding van Baäl.'

'Niet alle mensen, Elisa,' antwoordde zijn vader. 'Jou en mij niet.'

Elia stond op een verlaten, wankel altaar en keek langdurig naar

Elijah appeared
before King
Ahab and
commanded him
to gather all
Israel at Mount
Carmel.

father up the steep path. 'Let us pray that Elijah puts an end to
his wickedness today. Jezebel and Ahab have frightened all Israel
into worshipping Baal.'

'Not all, Elisha,' replied his father. 'Not you and me.'

Elijah stood on an abandoned, crumbling altar of the Lord
God and looked intently at the huge crowd of awestruck
Israelites.

'How long will you go limping along?' he demanded.
'Staggering between two different beliefs? If the Lord is God,
then follow Him.' Condemnation flashed in his eyes as he
looked at the priests of Baal. 'But if Baal is god, then follow
him.'

The people shifted uneasily. Most of them had indeed taken
to worshipping Baal.

'I alone am left!' Elijah roared. 'One prophet of the Lord!
But Baal's priests are four hundred and fifty.' He turned towards
the prophets and said, 'Let two bulls be given to us! Make an
altar to your...your Baal, prepare your sacrifice, but set no fire
to it. Then call on the name of your god! And I will call on the

name of my God. The one who answers by fire, let Him be the true God!'

Inspired by Elijah's words, the people raised their fists in the air and cheered.

The priests of Baal danced and sang before their altar. Louder and louder they chanted, faster and faster they whirled. Their hands clawed at the sky, as if to draw down fire from the sun.

Elijah inspected their tinder-dry altar. 'Call him harder,' he mocked. 'Perhaps he is lost in thought or he is away on a long journey? Perhaps he has fallen asleep. Call him!'

The priests danced until they staggered with exhaustion, until they grew hoarse and could call no more.

Then Elijah began to repair the neglected altar of the Lord God. The people rushed forward to help. Finally, the second bull was set upon the great cairn of stones.

'Now drench the sacrifice,' Elijah commanded.

Water was carried all the way up the mountain and poured over the altar until it was saturated. Then Elijah knelt before the

At Mount Carmel, Elijah challenged the priests of Baal.

En toen ontstak het altaar in vlammen.

Achab en alle andere mensen vielen in ontzag ter aarde. Alleen Elia bleef staan.

'Grijp alle profeten van Baäl,' zei hij met donderende stem, 'en dood hen!'

De mensen kwamen als één man overeind en joegen de vierhonderdvijftig priesters van Baäl naar een groot ravijn. De profeten riepen Baäl aan en smeekten voor hun leven. Maar Baäl kon hen net zomin helpen als dat hij een vuur kon laten ontbranden.

Toen vormden zich donkere wolken in de lucht. Voor het eerst in drie jaar begon het te regenen.

Het altaar brandt met prachtige vlammen.

De regen kwam in steeds grotere hoeveelheden naar beneden en doordrenkte de opgeheven gezichten van de menigte. Elia strekte zijn hand uit naar Achab.

'Neem je strijdwagens mee en verdwijn!' beval hij. Triomfantelijk keek hij toe hoe de gestrafte koning zich terughaastte naar Izebel. Hij haalde diep adem. De wind die vanuit Samaria waaide rook fris en schoon alsof alle angst weggespoeld was.

Elia begon de berg af te dalen, naar de wildernis die zijn thuis was. Hij had de Hebreeërs laten zien dat de Here nog altijd de enige God was. Meer kon hij niet doen.

De profeten van Baäl worden in het ravijn gegooid.

crowd, Elijah stretched out his hand towards Ahab.

'Take your chariots and go!' he commanded.

Elijah watched in triumph as the chastened King hurried back to Jezebel. He breathed deeply. The wind which blew in from Samaria smelled clean and fresh, as if all fear had been washed away.

Elijah began to walk down the mountain, towards the wasteland that was his home. He had shown the Hebrews that the Lord was still the only God. He could do no more.

When Ahab told her what Elijah had done, Jezebel was furious.

When Ahab arrived at the palace Jezebel was chanting praises to Baal, thanking him for the rain.

'Elijah,' he whined, not daring to meet his wife's eye. 'Elijah

has murdered your prophets.'

Jezebel froze. 'He has slain the priests of my lord Baal?'

'It was at the word of the prophet Elijah,' Ahab mumbled.

Jezebel's eyes glittered with wrath, 'Then send the word of the priestess of Baal to Elijah the "prophet"! Say: may the gods have their revenge on me if I do not have my revenge on him!'

Ahab remembered the cheers of the crowd. 'But...the people...' he stuttered, afraid that they might turn on him as they had turned on the priests.

'The people?' Jezebel echoed scornfully. 'Are you the King of Israel or is Elijah's power greater than yours?'

And so, once again, Ahab ordered his soldiers out into the country to search for Elijah. Through rain and hail they marched from house to house, farm to farm, looking for the last prophet of the Lord God.

At last they came to the farm of Elisha's father. When Elisha learned why they were looking for the holy prophet, he quietly set down his tools and wandered off. When he was sure that he had not attracted the soldiers' attention, he slipped away from the farm and set off for the wilderness to warn Elijah.

He came upon the holy man huddled in a simple shelter on a rain-swept hillside.

When Elijah heard that Jezebel's word was still law, that it was on her orders that the soldiers were seeking to take his life, his heart sank. Despite having seen God's fire with his own eyes, Ahab had allowed this to happen. Baal was still god in Israel.

Even so far from Samaria he sensed the stink of fear.

'She seeks my life to destroy it?' Elijah sighed. He shook his head. 'What is my life? After all I have done, nothing has changed. Where is the Lord God of Israel? Where is His power?'

Elisha tried to protest but Elijah would not listen.

Elisa waarschuwt
Elia dat Izebel
zich wil wreken.

En terwijl Elia sliep stuurde de Here God zijn engelen om in dit uur van wanhoop naast hem te zitten.

'Deze lange reis is te zwaar voor je,' fluisterden de engelen. 'Veel te zwaar.'

Maar toen de uitgeputte man langzaam wakker werd, begonnen ze te fluisteren: 'Sta op en eet, Elia. Sta op en eet.'

Eenmaal wakker voelde Elia zich eigenaardig getroost. En toen hij een vuur zag waarop brood voor hem was gebakken om hem te versterken, net als in Sarfat, wist hij dat hij niet alleen was. En toen hij een kan met koel water zag staan om hem nieuwe kracht te geven, wist hij dat de Here God nog werk voor zijn laatste profeet had.

'Ga naar Sinaï en beklim de berg om voor het aangezicht van God te verschijnen.' De woorden kwamen uit een doornenstruik die siste van de vlammen.

Sinaï? Elia voelde zich overweldigd. God bedoelde de ver weg gelegen berg Sinaï waar Mozes de stem van God had gehoord, waar God de Hebreeërs de geboden had gegeven. Wat wilde God van Elia op die plek?

strength, he knew that the Lord God still had work for His last prophet to do.

'*Go up to Sinai and stand there on the mount before the Lord.*' The word sang out from the thorn bush, sizzled from the fire.

Sinai? Elijah was overwhelmed. It was on faraway Mount Sinai that Moses had heard God's voice, there that God had given the Hebrews their laws. What could the Lord want with Elijah in such a place?

Elijah left Israel and walked night and day until he came to the distant mountain. With the last of his strength he dragged himself up to the great rock face at the top.

The desert wind gathered its force and howled around him. He pressed himself into a cleft in the rock, gasping for breath in the face of the great tempest. The ground began to quake and split beneath his feet. Elijah cried out in terror. And then the

Elijah climbed to the top of Mount Sinai.

earth and the air stood still and a great sheet of flame engulfed the mountain and died away without scorching a blade of grass or a hair of Elijah's head. The Lord was here – but the word was not.

In anguish, Elijah fell to his knees and waited.

Night came. The world stayed very still. The word did not come bounding from the rock beneath him, nor from the sky above. Instead there came a voice, a true voice. It pierced the air, a small, still voice as clear as a hammer ringing on iron.

'Elijah....'

It was the voice of God Himself.

Elijah trembled with fear.

'What are you doing here, Elijah?' asked God kindly.

'Oh...Lord...I....' A sweet, clear light enfolded him.

He shielded his eyes, overwhelmed by the closeness of the Lord his God. 'I...have been very jealous for the Lord God of Hosts,' he explained hesitantly. 'For the children of Israel have forgotten your promises, thrown down your altars and slain your prophets with their swords. And I...I am the only one left – and now they want to take my life away.'

'What are you doing here, Elijah?' God asked again.

Elijah began to weep. How could he answer when he could no longer be sure?

'Go now,' God said. 'For you shall declare my judgment on the house of Ahab, and you shall anoint Elisha, the son of Shaphat, to be a prophet in your place.'

Elijah's heart leapt. No longer would Ahab take bread from the mouths of the Hebrews, force them to kneel before idols, torment and twist and torture the very people he was meant to lead. And when Ahab had been told of the Lord's judgment, Elijah could set down his burden. God had chosen another to bear its weight, to continue His work.

'I have left myself seven thousand followers in Israel,' God reassured him. 'All the faithful who have not bowed to Baal, and every mouth which has not kissed him.'

Seven thousand? Elijah closed his eyes and smiled. So he was not alone, after all.

The journey back to Israel was long, but Elijah undertook it with a light heart. He arrived at last in the fertile valley where Elisha lived, and found the young man ploughing.

Elijah took off his mantle and swept it across Elisha's face. 'The spirit of the Lord God shall rest upon you,' he said. Then he put it back on his shoulders, turned, and walked away.

Elisha ran to his family and threw down his own mantle. He started to follow Elijah.

'You are my firstborn son,' his father protested. 'When I divide the inheritance you will have the double portion.'

But Elisha could not choose his family over God. His father saw this in his son's eyes, and understood. As Elisha ran to join Elijah, the old man smiled with pride.

'What have I done to you?' Elijah sighed as he saw how eager

Elisha was ploughing his fields when Elijah returned to the valley.

Elijah and Elisha
found the King
in a vineyard.

Elisha was to take on this terrible burden. 'Are you not afraid
of the King of Israel and his armies?'

'I fear only the Lord God of Israel,' said Elisha.

'Then you *are* the one,' responded Elijah gratefully.

Together they went in search of Ahab. They found the King
stretched out in the moonlight in a vineyard, eating grapes.

'Thus says the Lord,' pronounced Elijah as he stood in front
of the frightened King. 'Because you have killed the prophets
of the land, robbed the poor of their inheritance and murdered
the innocent, I will sweep you away, you and all your
descendants.'

Ahab almost choked on his terror as he saw the truth in
Elijah's eyes.

The prophesy was not long in coming true.

As Ahab prepared to fight a battle against the Syrians, he remembered Elijah's words and shivered. Many arrows would be aimed at him this day because he was king. He went into battle dressed as a common soldier, believing that his disguise would save his life. But it did not. The Lord God was not deceived.

Elijah's work was finished. He set off across the desert. 'Stay here,' he told Elisha. 'For the word of the Lord has come to me again and sent me to Jordan.'

'I will not leave you,' Elisha insisted.

Elijah travelled onwards with Elisha at his side.

'The King is dead, but what about the Queen?' Elisha asked.

'Her time has not yet come,' said Elijah. It would be many months before she died, at the hands of a vengeful slave.

At last the two men reached the river Jordan. 'You must leave now,' said Elijah, but Elisha refused to go.

So Elijah walked boldly down the banks of the river, with Elisha stumbling behind him. At the edge of the water Elijah stopped and held out his mantle as if wielding a sword. To Elisha's astonishment the waters heaved themselves apart, creating a pathway for them to cross.

On the far side, beyond the valley, loomed the great cliffs of the wilderness which had for so long been Elijah's home.

'What do you want me to do for you,' Elijah asked the young man beside him, 'before I am taken from you?'

'Father,' Elisha replied, 'let me inherit a double portion of your spirit.'

'You have asked me the hardest thing,' Elijah said gently. 'Yet if you see me as I am taken from you, it shall be so. But if you do not see me, it shall not be so.'

Elijah walked on, through the green pastures of the valley towards the barren land.

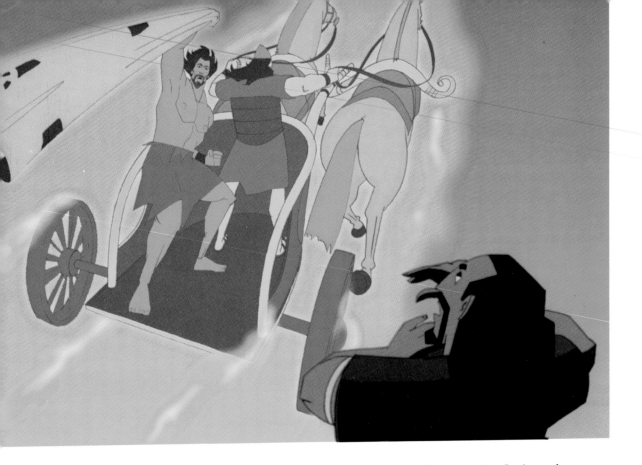

Elijah was
carried up to
God by the fiery
Chariot of Israel.

And then, suddenly, the sky was filled with flailing hooves, and the air flared with a great light. Fiery horses were drawing a fiery chariot down from heaven to gather up Elijah and take him home to the Lord God.

'The Chariot of Israel and its horsemen!' cried Elisha, looking up.

Joy burned in Elijah's eyes as he was swept away. As the horses galloped higher and higher, Elijah tore off his mantle and sent it spiralling down to Elisha.

The young man held it, hardly daring to believe that it was truly his. Then, when he reached the river bank, he was struck by a sudden panic. 'Where is the Lord, the God of Elijah?' he cried.

With a shaking hand he held out the mantle as Elijah had done. The waters parted to speed him home.

DANIEL

aniel's heart thudded in time to the pounding on the city walls. He gripped the hilt of his sword. 'Surely the walls can't take much more of this?'

'Jerusalem will belong to the Babylonians before this night is out,' his friend replied.

'Not if I have anything to do with it,' Daniel said fiercely. 'I'll fight to the death to save my city.'

'We all will,' Mishael reminded him. 'But there are so many of them, so few of us.'

Daniel swallowed hard. 'But if we pray, with the Lord God's help....'

'I'm praying already,' replied Mishael, sharply. 'But the Lord God doesn't always want for us what we want for ourselves.'

At midnight the city walls of Jerusalem broke. Flaming

The invading Babylonian soldiers stole the sacred objects from the temple of Jerusalem.

torches streamed through the breach like a river of light.

Daniel and his fellow Hebrews hurled themselves at the invading soldiers. They battled bravely, but it was hopeless. The massive Babylonian army had stolen yet another city for their vast empire. And having stolen Jerusalem, the Babylonians proceeded to steal every precious thing in it. They even took the sacred objects from the temple. Then they captured every man, woman or child who looked healthy enough to make a good slave. And finally, from the comfort of their chariots, they forced the Hebrews to march many hundreds of miles across the desert to Babylon. The journey was long and hard, and many died along the way. As the city of Babylon loomed, Daniel turned to his three friends who marched alongside him.

'We are supposed to be leaders of the Hebrews,' he said bitterly, 'but instead we are watching them being led into slavery.'

'We are slaves ourselves now,' said Mishael. 'What choice do we have?'

'No wonder the Babylonians are so powerful,' Hananiah remarked. 'Just look at the scale of those city walls, all the towers....'

'The buildings don't impress me,' muttered Azariah. 'Anyone could have a city this size if they used slave labour.'

Once inside Babylon's walls, Daniel and Mishael, Hananiah and Azariah, were separated from the rest of the captives and taken to the palace of King Nebuchadnezzar.

The King studied them. 'These are the four princes you told me about?'

'Yes, your Majesty,' the captain of his guard replied.

'Hmmm....' He beckoned the four young men over. 'I'm going to have you trained up,' he announced, catching the eye of his son, Belshazzar. He had often told Belshazzar that

captives were easier to control if you gave their leaders positions of importance. He hoped that the young man would remember this when it was his turn to be king.

'You shall work for me as magi,' Nebuchadnezzar told the Hebrews. 'You will advise me, govern the provinces, foretell the future, interpret sacrifices to the gods....'

Daniel's eyes widened with disgust. He had heard about the so-called gods that the Babylonians worshipped. They were nothing but carved statues, graven images! The sooner the Babylonians turned to the one true God the better. 'But, your Majesty,' he exclaimed, horrified, 'we cannot serve your gods! If your rituals demand that—'

'Daniel!' hissed Hananiah. 'Shhhh....'

'We usually allow three years to train a magus,' the King continued, ignoring Daniel's protest. 'If you're not adequate by then...you die.'

Daniel turned to his friends, aghast, and lowered his voice. 'How can we have anything to do with these gods?' he demanded.

Mishael gazed helplessly at him. 'Look at our people.' He pointed to a window. Outside, a group of Hebrews were being man-handled by their new masters. 'We must accept this...this honour,' he whispered. 'Use it to do what we can for them.'

'I can learn the skills of a magus,' admitted Daniel, reluctantly. 'But if they ask me to deny the Lord God, to break His laws, then I cannot.'

Although he was as appalled as Daniel, Mishael said nothing more until they were alone in their apartments. He understood how foolish it would be to stir things up before they had to. They could not help their people if they were dead.

As the months dragged by, the four young men studied hard and prayed hard. Ashpenaz, the steward of the palace, began to admire them, and even Belshazzar enjoyed their company. He was fascinated by their Lord God. 'This one God, he does everything?' he asked Daniel.

'He protects us. One God is all a man needs.'

'And he never loses his temper with you?'

'As long as we obey His laws.'

'But does he reveal the future to you?'

'If that is what is required. But it's not important. As long as He is obeyed, the future will be safe.'

Belshazzar was irritated by Daniel's answers. What was the point of a god who would not reveal the future? Or one who was such a stickler about obedience, come to that?

Then one day, Ashpenaz burst into the princes' apartment and announced that they had been especially chosen by King Nebuchadnezzar to share his meat. 'It comes straight from the temple of the god Marduk,' he revealed. 'Only the most honoured share the King's meat.'

Daniel winced. 'Then the meat has been part of a sacrifice?'

Ashpenaz nodded eagerly.

Ashpenaz burst
into the
apartment to
offer the four
Hebrew princes
the honour of
sharing the
King's meat.

'Then we cannot accept it.' Daniel was adamant. 'Our God will not let us. This meat has been offered to another god – tainted by his ritual.'

Belshazzar snorted. 'No reasonable god would ask you to refuse such an honour!' he jeered as he stormed out.

'There's no other food for me to give you,' Ashpenaz protested. 'And when you get sick, I will be punished.'

'We will manage without food,' Daniel insisted. 'In time you will see, we will be none the worse for it.'

To his surprise, Ashpenaz found himself agreeing to Daniel's request – even though he would be in terrible trouble if he was discovered. He did not know what was happening to him lately. Why was he so eager to please this determined young man?

Amazingly, after ten days on dry crusts, water and a great deal of prayer, the four Hebrews looked healthier than they had done at the outset.

Nonetheless, when Nebuchadnezzar and his retinue swept into the Hebrews' apartment, Ashpenaz' heart thudded with terror.

'I want to see how your studies are coming along,' the King declared. 'I hear good things, don't I, Lord Magus?'

The Lord Magus, who was the King's chief advisor, narrowed his eyes and stared at the four young men. He had heard a rumour concerning the princes and the meat, and was hoping the King would put them to death for their disobedience – especially Daniel, who was staring boldly back.

But Nebuchadnezzar only said, 'You're looking very well. The temple meat obviously suits you.' Then he asked to see some of their work.

Daniel handed him the astrological charts he had been drawing up.

'Most impressive,' said Nebuchadnezzar, admiringly. He handed them to the Lord Magus.

'They're adequate,' the Lord Magus muttered, disgusted that the Hebrews should be praised instead of being punished.

'The Lord God leads us,' Daniel explained.

'He leads you well,' said the King. 'Now what about the treasury figures?'

Daniel handed his calculations to the King.

Nebuchadnezzar studied them delightedly. 'Very good. *Very good*. I can't see any point in training you any more.'

The Lord Magus was enraged. How dare these foreigners learn his skills so quickly – and so well! 'Your Majesty,' he said through clenched teeth, 'surely there is still much —'

'I appoint you all full king's magi. Get them their proper robes, Ashpenaz!'

Full magi? The Lord Magus ground his teeth. It had taken him years and years to become a full magi! Daniel was no more than a boy!

As the King left, he turned to the Lord Magus. 'They'll be teaching you soon,' he chuckled.

The Magus glared furiously at Daniel. This slave boy might have impressed the King, but he would make the Israelite pay dearly for his arrogance one of these days....

Daniel set about his work determinedly, delighted to have the chance to help his people. But then something happened which made the Lord Magus hate Daniel even more.

The King suffered the same nightmare for three nights in a row. He called all the magi to his chamber and demanded an interpretation.

The Lord Magus preened himself. 'Of course, your Majesty,' he oozed. 'Tell me the dream and I shall interpret.'

King Nebuchadnezzar called all the magi for an interpretation of his dream.

Nebuchadnezzar was infuriated by the man's manner. 'No,' he scowled. 'How do I know you have these powers? First you must tell me the dream.' He glared at the bewildered Lord Magus and then stared challengingly at the rest. 'Come on,' he urged. 'Any of you?'

'But Majesty,' protested the Lord Magus. 'No mortal can know another's dream. None of us —'

'Do not refuse me!' roared the King. 'Guards! Have all the magi executed.'

Every magus in the palace was imprisoned that night. The executions were to take place at dawn.

As the frightened Hebrew princes were being led to their cell they prayed to the Lord God for help, and they prayed without ceasing all through the long night.

Just before dawn, images came into Daniel's mind. Sensing that this might be the answer to his prayer, he demanded to be taken to Nebuchadnezzar's room. He was marched there by a guard, followed anxiously by the Lord Magus.

Nebuchadnezzar stared coldly at Daniel.

The young man clenched his fists to still their trembling. If he was wrong, if his images were not a vision of the dream, then he would die a far more horrible death than the other magi.

'You...you watched,' began Daniel anxiously. 'You saw a huge tree, tall, still growing, strong, vibrant, topmost branches touching the clouds.'

Nebuchadnezzar said nothing.

'The tree fed everyone,' Daniel went on. 'And it shaded and sheltered the animals, gave a home to the birds.'

The King leant forward a little.

'And this tree, your Majesty, is you, providing for all the people of the earth.'

At that Nebuchadnezzar beamed.

'But then a Watcher, a Holy Watcher, came down from heaven. He cried, "Chop the tree down. The animals must run, the birds fly."'

Daniel took a deep breath then continued staunchly, 'You have risen too high, your Majesty, and the Lord God must bring you down. But the Watcher also said, "Leave the stump in the ground, bind him with iron rings, he can live in the rain with the beasts of the fields."' Daniel added, 'No longer human, you will have the mind of a beast for seven years.'

The King's smile disappeared.

'But there is hope,' Daniel persisted. 'The Watcher allowed the stump to live, did not uproot it. And when you come to acknowledge my God after those seven years, you will be restored to humanity.'

Daniel described a huge tree in the King's dream.

The men in the room exchanged horrified glances. 'Shall I kill him now, your Majesty?' asked the guard, reaching for his sword.

But Nebuchadnezzar was shaking with laughter. 'I have never heard anything quite so preposterous!' he howled. 'I knew you were different, Israelite. You are very special.'

'Who could possibly have such an absurd dream!' the Lord Magus scoffed.

'No,' returned Nebuchadnezzar, sharply. 'The dream was exactly as he said. And for that reason you shall all be saved. But...' And then he smirked and chuckled again, '...the interpretation. Too ridiculous for words!'

Daniel looked angrily at the King. Nebuchadnezzar clearly thought the whole thing was a joke.

A year passed. One day the King was in the grounds of the palace, gazing out over his city, when he spied Daniel.

'Aren't I supposed to be a donkey now?' he taunted. 'Or was it a giraffe? Or a crocodile?'

'I am only a voice for the Lord God,' Daniel replied truthfully.

'Look, Israelite,' The King's voice was full of contempt. 'Look at my city – why should I become an animal? I built this city!'

'As did a million captive slaves, including my people.'

'No, Israelite,' snorted the King. '*I built it!* Only I built Babylon, the greatest city the world has ever seen.'

But as he said it, his shoulders began to hunch and his back

'I built this city!' said the King.

The King began to change into a wild animal.

began to arch and his voice thickened and grew round and bellowing.

'What's happening to me…?' he growled, gazing at his fists which had been gripped by a spasm so severe that they seemed more like hooves than hands. 'I am the King!' he roared, but the words were rough-edged and hoarse.

'I am King Nebuchadnezzar….' he tried to say, but all that came out was the baying of a wild animal. He fell to his knees in horror.

The courtiers stared at him. What should they do? They could not treat this…this creature as a king. Nebuchadnezzar was crawling around on all fours!

The Lord Magus glanced at Belshazzar. Then a sly smile curled his lips. *He* knew what to do. He snatched the crown from Nebuchadnezzar's head and handed it to Belshazzar. 'Your Majesty,' he crooned in an oily voice.

Only Daniel did not bow to the new King. Instead, he crouched beside the pathetic old man and tried to comfort him.

'Remember, with faith you can come to the Lord God and be

restored,' Daniel whispered.

But Nebuchadnezzar only looked at Daniel with clouded, uncomprehending eyes.

'We no longer require your service at court, Israelite,' called Belshazzar. 'We were once friends. Be grateful to keep your life.'

Triumph glittered in the Lord Magus' eyes as he watched Daniel walk away.

As the years went by, Daniel tended the old King as best he could. And after seven years Nebuchadnezzar did indeed acknowledge the Lord God and was restored to sanity. But he could not govern his empire again. Belshazzar was enjoying being king far too much to return the crown – although he did far more feasting that he did governing. Under his slipshod rule, the great Babylonian Empire began to decay.

But Belshazzar did not care. Why should he? His god, Marduk, told him that everything was going to be all right.

Wine, women and wooden gods filled the great hall. Hearing the raucous laughter that signalled yet another feast, Daniel first prayed, then marched to the throne room to protest in the name of the Lord God.

Daniel's scathing countenance annoyed Belshazzar even more than his unexpected appearance. It was about time someone wiped that righteous expression off the Israelite's face.

With a sly smile, Belshazzar sent for the sacred, holy cups that had been stolen from the temple in Jerusalem. Then, in front of Daniel's shocked face, he had them filled with wine and made his friends drink toasts from them – toasts to Marduk and all the other delightful little Babylonian gods who foretold the future and did not give two hoots for obedience. Ha! Serve the Israelite right!

For a time, everyone cheered and laughed and sloshed wine into the sacred vessels. But then, abruptly, the laughter stopped.

A point of light had appeared, hovering over the wall behind Belshazzar. The light grew thick and solid and turned into a human hand. The Babylonians watched in terror as the hand wrote four words on the wall and then shrivelled to a pin-prick of fading light.

'Magus!' yelled the petrified Belshazzar. 'Magus!'

The Lord Magus came rushing up and peered at the writing.

'Read it,' urged Belshazzar, feverishly, 'and you'll have riches beyond any man's dreams – gold, silver, frankincense…. Anything.'

'Er, it looks like….'

But no matter how lavish the bribes, no matter how desperately he tried to salvage his dignity, the humiliated Lord Magus could not read the words.

Belshazzar became frantic.

Daniel stepped forward. 'Would your Majesty like to hear the interpretation?'

Suddenly, handwriting appeared on the wall behind Belshazzar.

The huge army
of the Medes
broke through
the city walls of
Babylon.

'You can read it? Everything I've offered—'

'Keep your gifts,' Daniel said coldly. Then he approached the
wall and pointed at the words. '"Mene, mene..." – the Lord
God has numbered the days of your reign and brought it to an
end. "Tekel..." – you have been weighed in the balance and
found wanting. "U-pharsin..." – your kingdom has been
divided amongst the Medes and the Persians.'

'How dare he?' blazed the Lord Magus. 'How dare this
foreigner insult the King of Babylon in this way? This is our
king. And who are you? An Israelite! A hostage! Don't listen to
him, your Majesty, it's nonsense.'

But it was not nonsense. At that very moment Darius, the
King of the Medes, was leading a huge army into the city. The
undisciplined Babylonian guards scrambled for their arms and
tried to repel the invaders, but the Medes were too numerous
and too powerful to be overthrown.

A guard came to Belshazzar, his sword drawn and
bloodstained. 'The Medes are inside the city walls!' he cried.
'What shall we do?'

Darius, the new
ruler of Babylon,
grew to like
Daniel more and
more.

The King stumbled to his feet. 'My sword, my shield,' he ordered weakly. 'We will fight.'

But even as he said it his eyes were drawn to the writing on the wall and he knew that the battle was lost.

Within hours, Darius, King of the Medes, was the new ruler of Babylon. To establish his authority he put Belshazzar and many of the courtiers to death, but he allowed the magi to live, knowing, as Nebuchadnezzar had known before him, that he would need help to rule this huge empire of slaves successfully.

One magus was to be given the vital job of City Governor. Darius chose Daniel.

Bile rose in the Lord Magus' throat. The Israelite had been chosen over him? It was the final humiliation. He vowed that he would not rest until he had taken his revenge on Daniel.

As time passed, Darius grew to like Daniel more and more. Daniel was an excellent governor, hard working and fair. Under his rule Babylon prospered – and so did the Hebrew captives, many of whom had risen to become skilled craftsmen.

'Your people are resilient,' Darius remarked.

'They have to be, your Highness,' returned Daniel.

Darius frowned. The same could be said of all the other captives in the city, but none of them had done so well for themselves. 'Just what is the source of this strength?' he asked.

'Knowing that we will return to our homeland one day,' explained Daniel. 'And that the Lord God's reign will be established on earth.'

'I admire your people, Daniel.'

Daniel turned pleading eyes on the King. 'Then why keep us all hostages? Why keep us here?'

'If I freed the Israelites,' Darius said firmly, 'this whole empire would collapse. Let one tribe go free – it is the end.'

'And yet you allow us to worship the one true God who will one day destroy all earthly empires?'

'Oh, worship who you want. I don't care. It's order I want.'

The Lord Magus wanted order too. He wanted the sort of order which would place him at the top and Daniel in his grave. But how? How could he disgrace a man who was so close to the King? The Lord Magus had influence within the palace, but Daniel governed the entire city.

And then one day, the Lord Magus saw Daniel at his prayers and had an idea.

He hurried gleefully to the throne room. 'Highness!' he proclaimed. 'The sacrifices have spoken! Holy Marduk has made his wishes plain. For the next thirty days, no citizen must petition any man or god except you. Anyone who disobeys will be thrown into the royal lion pit.'

'Me?' Darius could not help but be flattered that a god had selected him for this honour.

'No one but the King should receive petitions,' the Lord
Magus continued. 'It must be decreed.'

Hananiah, Daniel's friend, was still one of the court magi and
heard what was said. He understood immediately what the
Lord Magus was planning, and hurried to warn Daniel.

Daniel arrived in the throne room just as the royal seal was
about to be applied to the decree. He tried to protest that the
decree would outlaw his daily prayers to the Lord God,
that he could never obey such a law, but Darius was so
overwhelmed by the Lord Magus' pronouncement
that he paid no attention.

Daniel defied the
decree and began
to pray.

The seal was applied. The Lord Magus' scheme
was law.

'For thirty days', taunted the Lord Magus, 'you
must make no prayer to any other god except his
Highness.'

Daniel's face burned. He marched
determinedly to his room. The entire court
hurried to the courtyard and looked up at
Daniel's window. Within a few minutes Daniel
appeared. The onlookers held their breath.
Surely he would not pray openly, in front of so
many witnesses?

Daniel turned to face Jerusalem.

Then, in full view of the King, he began to
pray to the Lord his God.

Darius watched in horror as his most valued
friend flouted the law. He understood now why
Daniel had tried to stop him, but it was too late.
For order to prevail, the King must be obeyed.
'Arrest him,' he said wearily.

As Daniel was led to the lion pit,

Darius waited for him.

'You can still tell me you were not praying,' he urged Daniel, but he knew as he said it that Daniel would never lie about such a matter.

'"Worship who you want,"' retorted Daniel. 'That's what you said.'

'I was misled.'

'So was I.'

The flagstone covering the lion pit was lifted. They could smell the lions, see the hunger in their yellow eyes. The animals had not been fed for days.

As Daniel looked down on the famished, snarling beasts, Darius said uncertainly, 'Your God will protect you.'

Daniel nodded.

'I will pray for you, Daniel,' promised the white-faced Darius.

As his friend descended into the pit, Darius saw the lions flex their claws and bare their teeth. He heard them growl softly, dangerously, as they fixed their eyes on their prey.

Then the stone was replaced, not to be lifted again until dawn broke.

Darius kept his word. Immediately, he began to pray to the Lord God in whom Daniel trusted.

And down amongst the ravenous, pacing lions Daniel also prayed.

All night long, while the Lord Magus gloated, Darius fasted and prayed. When the stone was lifted, Darius could not bear to look.

'Highness?' It was Daniel's voice, echoing up from below.

Darius rushed to the entrance and watched Daniel climb the steps.

Daniel smiled. 'I think the lions may be a little hungry!'

'Are you hurt?' Darius asked anxiously.

'No. The Lord God sent an angel to still the lions. I did you no injury, your Highness. The lion did me no injury.'

Darius let out a shaky sigh of relief. He was just about to lead Daniel off to celebrate when he noticed rage in the Lord Magus' eye and suddenly understood how he had been tricked. 'Arrest him,' he commanded, pointing at the Lord Magus. 'Tomorrow *he* shall feed the lions.'

Daniel protested, but Darius would not relent.

So Daniel did the only thing that was left to him. He lifted his eyes to heaven. 'Oh, Lord God,' he prayed, weary of this endless bloodshed. 'We pray for mercy and forgiveness for all, and for deliverance for all people everywhere.'

'Your Lord God answered my prayer,' said Darius. 'He will answer yours, I am sure.'

'Will He?' Daniel met Darius' eye. 'You will not deliver my people from slavery, will you?'

'No,' said Darius. 'But I will send out a decree to the whole empire, commanding everyone to worship your Lord God.'

A look of wonder and delight spread across Daniel's face. The carved statues would be banished from this great empire! The Lord God would reign in Babylon!

'Are you not angry with me?' Darius asked in surprise.

'God does not always want for us what we want for ourselves,' Daniel explained. 'Just now, He wants all the people of this empire to know that He is the one true God, and for that He delivered me from the lions. But the day will come when He takes us home to Israel again, you can be sure of that. Until then we must obey Him and wait.'